AF264640

ISBN 978-0-578-65761-5 (Hardcover Edition)
ISBN 978-0-578-65712-7 (Softcover Edition)

Printed in the United States of America

First Printing June 2020

Published by Conron Books

Clamdigger

Childhood Stories

Anita LeClaire Conron

Clamming at low tide in Rhode Island, 1856
Courtesy of the Rhode Island Historical Society
RHi X17 2404 Albumen print, Wm. Mills & Son

If you resided in Riverside, Rhode Island, you were a *Clamdigger.* You did not have to dig them or even eat one to be a recipient of that title, you only had to live there.

Riverside was bordered on the west by miles of waterways. This geographic happenstance was the ideal setting for the habitation of those tender, succulent sea creatures called Little Neck Clams, hence the title *Clamdigger*.

I lived with my father, mother, and sisters: Mary and Alicia. Mary was born 18 months before me, and Alicia nine years my junior. Riverside, Rhode Island, was my home until I left to be married.

Mary always said if you looked up Riverside in the dictionary the definition would read: *Boring.* I didn't agree. I loved where we lived and was convinced we had as much adventure, intrigue, suspense, and just plain fun as any place on the planet.

They were years of innocence. The community was my world. For me, growing up in the nineteen forties and fifties were days that were simple, secure, and brimming with interesting and entertaining people for me to observe.

These stories are about my childhood. I was a daydreamer and watched, with curiosity and wonder, as exciting, endless, tales of daily life unfolded.

Acknowledgements

My family, friends, and neighbors were the incentive to create and develop these childhood stories. I thank them for making my growing-up years happy and full of adventure.

I am grateful to my memoirs writing instructor, Richard Ohler. He encouraged me, for the past eighteen years, to explore my past experiences and put them down on paper. He guided me along the way with thoughtful, constructive criticism to help me become a better writer. I also thank my fellow writers in our memoirs class.

A special thanks to my sisters, Mary McCarthy and Alicia LeClaire, for jogging my memory when necessary and providing love and constant support.

My cousin, Michael Reynolds, provided me with many necessary genealogical facts. He was patient with my repeated requests for information.

My cousin, Tom Reynolds, revealed an unknown story to me about what he learned from my Uncle Ed and how it remains a beautiful gift that he still enjoys today.

Thanks to Chris Burke who edited some of my early stories. She was a good-natured, valuable tutor.

This book would never have materialized if it had not been for the capable, loving, unfailing knowledge and guidance of two remarkable women: Anna Davidson and Debby Sullivan. Anna formatted all my stories, photographs, and knew her way around the mysteries of desktop publishing. Debby was my editor and with her trained eye discovered misspellings, grammatical errors, and content inconsistencies. They both worked together on this project in unapparelled unison. Anna and Debby made my journey fun and exciting. We became good friends. Ladies, you were my rock.

Table of Contents

* All sketches in this book were drawn by the author.

This collection of stories is

dedicated

to

my sons

Bill, Dan, Matt, and Tim

I hope they discover that I, too, was a child once upon a time.

Love, Mom

My Family

Family photo taken in 1943
My mother, Ronnie, my father, Leo,
me, born in 1938, and Mary, born in 1936. Baby Alicia arrived in 1947
and is shown here through the magic of Photoshop.

THE SILENT SALT MARSHES

Peaceful Waters

Each night I fell asleep listening to the cadence of the foghorn moaning its three-second warning to ships as they traveled through the narrows of Narragansett Bay and eventually out to the Atlantic Ocean. It is not surprising that the ocean, the bays, the marshes, and the inlets of Rhode Island continue to be a part of my being.

The salt marshes play a vital role in the ecosystem of this complex watery arena in and around Rhode Island. They are the spawning grounds for fish and a variety of shellfish. They stretch out along the rivers and bays and at times snuggle up to the banks and hug the shoreline, secure as a newborn to its mother.

The marshes first appear as mounds of rich brown soil entangled with roots, teaming with life, and hidden from view. Grasses adorn them, like topknots, standing tall and proud, stretching their razor-sharp tips skyward on a still, cloudless, summer day. The narrow green blades of grass wait patiently for a gentle breeze and the water's movement to redirect them. They are willing and graceful dancers.

Salt marshes often reach beyond the banks of the shoreline and stretch out in the distance, resembling a neglected overgrown pasture. During the fall and winter months the grassland turns from green to tan, sometimes appearing shriveled and lifeless. The dry grasses lie flat and struggle to right themselves as they are coached by a gust of bone-chilling winter wind. The old grass protects and nourishes the new shoots that will emerge with the approaching warm weather. It is our prairie.

I first started noticing the marshes on our Sunday family rides when I was about six. My father often headed our black Dodge out of Riverside, southeast, to the next town, Barrington. The road curved along the Barrington River mimicking each bend in the waterway.

In the distance I would occasionally see kids my age in a heavy wooden rowboat exploring the inlets. I watched the passing scene with my chin resting on the car window rim envisioning the rowboat's occupants not to be the two boys, but my best friend, Barbara, and me. We would sit amidships, each with an oar, laughing, revolving our craft in dizzying circles as we attempted to row out into the open waters of the channel.

Salt Marshes off Jamestown, RI
Photo: Bill Kiggen

Sometimes my dad made a left-hand turn over the bridge situated next to the white clapboard Barrington Congregational church. The roof of this stately house of worship boasted a steeple so tall and slender it appeared to be capable of piercing any passing cloud.

We entered the picturesque community of Hampton Meadows. Weathered Cape Cod homes and the occasional converted summer cottage sat comfortably nestled one next to another. Marshes sometimes appeared in the distance where a road dead-ended at the water and a sandy beach came into view.

I imagined the fun of walking down to the water in my bathing suit with a towel draped over my shoulder. I would kick up the dust from the road with my bare feet, then cleanse and cool them off in the Barrington River, enjoying my own private stretch of the seashore.

I loved those wetlands; they held secrets. Important, unseen things were happening in the dark world below the water's surface. The marshes are a place to dream and to imagine. They evolve with infinite beauty and purpose, always surprising and satisfying to the eye. In the silence of the salt marshes, I felt like I belonged.

Salt marshes produce more basic food energy per acre than any known ecosystem, including tropical rainforests and freshwater wetlands. Save the Bay, Narragansett Bay (RI) 1970.

Rhode Island

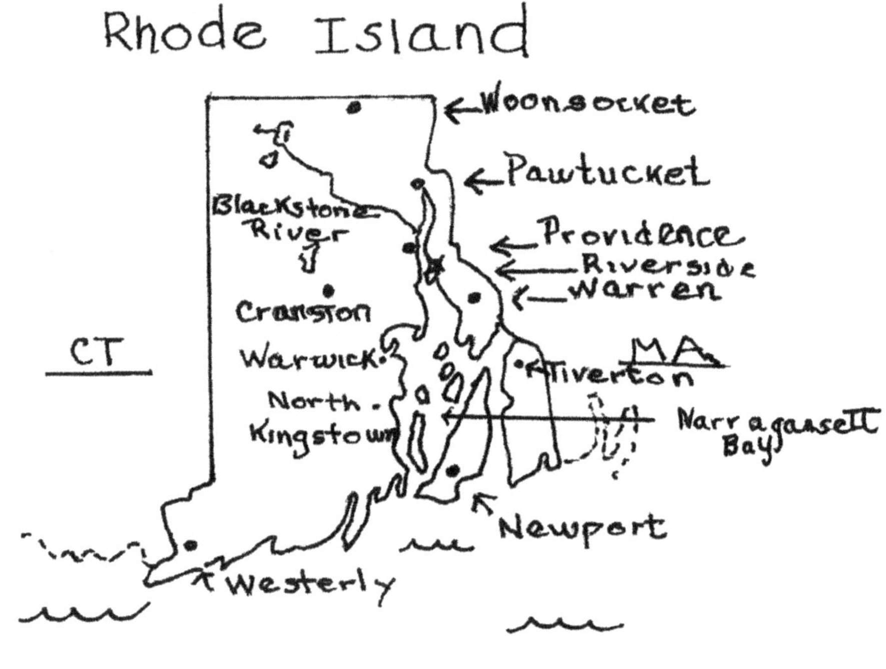

TOO CLOSE FOR COMFORT

Coping with a Rhode Island Summer

"It's a close one."

This expression might be used to describe the final heat of an exciting horse race, but it meant something entirely different if you resided in Riverside, Rhode Island, during the months of July and August. Hot, humid, and feeling uncomfortably close, was just the way things were.

My family lived in the middle of our town. We were far enough away from Narragansett Bay to maybe catch a rare breeze coming in off the water, so the weekends sometimes meant looking for respite from the unwelcome annual sticky weather. Those dog days of summer signaled an escape to the abundant beaches, lakes, and picnic grounds that made Rhode Island a nice place to live.

The Ocean State, Rhode Island and Providence Plantations (official name) was the last of the original thirteen colonies to become a state: the smallest in the union. Many of the beaches have retained their intriguing Native American names: Misquamicut, Weekapaug, and Quonochontaug, to name a few.

My favorite name was a lake and not a saltwater beach. My dad taught all three of his daughters to pronounce: Lake Chargoggagoggmanchauggagoggchaubunagungamaugg, the home of the Nipmuc Indians. This was also known as Lake Webster, located in Massachusetts near the Connecticut and Rhode Island border. The name, derived from the Algonquian language, means *fishing place at the boundaries-neutral meeting grounds.* A modern-day translation is easier to understand: *You fish on your side and I'll fish on my side and nobody fish in the middle.*

Sometimes our family summertime getaways involved a day trip north to Waterman Lake. Our Riverside neighbors, the Adams family, spent each summer in a house that Mr. Adams had built. It was an interesting structure right out of the pages of the British nursery rhyme: "The House that Jack Built." Additions just popped up, causing you to pause on the long path leading up to the house. It took a moment to spot the location of the main entrance every year.

Mr. Adams constructed a shed for boat oars and other gear, but we used it for a clubhouse. Their daughter, Nancy, my sister, Mary, and I made a sign and nailed it to the door that read: The Happy Secret Club. We never stayed in the little shed long enough for an official meeting since the small structure was devoid of windows and jammed with equipment making it unpleasant and stuffy. We soon tired of our dark, airless, crowded clubhouse and abandoned it for other activities, but I remember our little Happy Secret Club sign remaining on the door for years.

Mr. Adams and his inquisitive, friendly wife, Ruth, were always pleased to see us. Sometimes we walked down to the lake with Nancy for a swim and if we were lucky Nancy's older brother, Walt, came by to give us a spin around the lake, at breathtaking speed, in his high-powered motorboat.

We never tired of visiting my parents' best friends at their summer homes at Touisset Point or Hope Valley. We loved rowing down to the end of Locustville Pond at Hope Valley and gliding into the huge patch of seemingly endless white and yellow water lilies. I regularly leaned over the side of the boat and attempted to yank a water lily from its moorings. The long stems, slimy and tough, succeeded in never yielding to my act of bad behavior.

My parents had opportunities to purchase land for a summer place, but never did. In those days it was affordable. I think my mother did not like the idea of keeping up two homes. She told me that at one time they were about to buy some shore-front property south of us in Bay Springs prior to the 1938 hurricane. This storm devastated sections of the state. A few days following the hurricane, they went

Our house following the 1938 hurricane

to check on the land and discovered it had just vanished in the fury of the relentless wind and rain. My mother did talk about building an A-frame house up north near one of the lakes, but it never went beyond the talking stage.

Mother (Ronnie), me and, Mary at the beach, 1938

Some Sundays we drove to South County on the Connecticut side of the state to visit my mother's cousin, Kay Cawley Haggerty, who lived in a large farmhouse with her family a few miles from Matunuck Beach.

Matunuck Beach, barren and beautiful, facing Block Island Sound, had sand so hot you danced and hopped your way to the water. The blistering soles of your feet were soon forgotten as you immersed yourself into the refreshing, bone-chilling, icy waters of the Atlantic Ocean.

Their house, at the end of a long driveway, was surrounded by pastures that were divided into sections bordered by acres of stone walls. As the cows finished eating the grass in one pasture, they were then herded to the next grazing area, affording the old field time for new growth. We liked to climb to the second floor of their house and gaze out at the cows in the fields and the ocean in the distance.

Best of all was the farm itself. We spent lots of time sliding down the corn crib, until one day, Walter, Kay's husband, realizing what we were up to said,

"Be careful, girls, there are rats in the corn."

We never spotted one, but that was enough to discourage us from engaging in that sport again.

Some weekends we ventured down to the Newport beaches located on our side of the state and only a forty-five minute drive from home. The three public beaches were known by Rhode Islanders as First, Second, and Third, but to others unfamiliar with the area, as Easterns, Sachuest, and Navy. Many stretches of dunes and sandy beaches along the ocean, like those in Newport, were saved from development following the famous 1938 hurricane. People were reluctant to build near the water following that horrific storm. The state saw an opportunity and took over miles and miles of the Rhode Island shoreline, protecting those areas of unspoiled beauty forever.

Like so many others living close to the water, we enjoyed

Family picnic at Narragansett Beach, 1948

picnicking and swimming at the ocean. My mother always packed a sizable lunch in our brown metal picnic box. The inside container for ice never failed to leak and predictably turned a few sandwiches to mush. My father could repair just about anything and knew how to weld but, for some mysterious reason, never fixed the faulty, forever-dripping ice container.

The trips to the ocean did not happen as often as we would have liked because my mother did not enjoy being in the sun or wind with her sensitive, pale, Irish skin. I recall her sitting on a blanket under our butterscotch colored beach umbrella in a dress, even though she did own a pink, skirted, bathing suit. Sometimes she passed the time watching us from the shady side of our tent that my dad attached to one side of the car. Once when he purchased a new Dodge, a tent was included with each new vehicle as an added incentive. We loved the weighty, brown, canvas car tent. It served as a handy dressing room to change out of our swim clothes. My sisters and I slept in this favorite enclosure under the stars on many hot summer nights, camping out in our backyard.

We did not head to the water on all our weekend getaways. Sometimes we went to my grandmother's home in Rumford, only a few miles away. The house was at the very top of the hill on Dalton

Street so a nice breeze was guaranteed.

One warm Saturday afternoon my Uncle Ed came by to pick up my mother and my younger sister, Alicia, for a trip to Rumford. My father was away on business, so my sister, Mary, and I were planning on driving the family car there later, since we had summer jobs.

A day with the relatives was a good opportunity for us to show off the paper dresses Mary and I had recently purchased by mail order from *Seventeen* magazine for one dollar each. The horizontal striped narrow chemise dresses, in vivid shades of hot pink, lime green, canary yellow, and deep purples were, we thought, attractive and appealed to our sense of fashion. The dresses were cinched at the waist and neck with narrow plastic ties.

We donned our handsome, in vogue, paper attire by assisting each other in slipping them over our heads and securing the ties. The drive to my grandmother's on that hot sticky day, in our un-air-conditioned car, did cause us concern. We knew that to keep a fashion disaster at bay, it was imperative to stifle the urge to move and shift in the seat attempting to get more comfortable.

We drove up the gravel driveway and noticed everyone sitting in the shade of the grape arbor. We yelled out the open car window,

"We've got something neat to show you."

Mary and I attempted to leave the car, but the dresses refused to cooperate. They had adhered themselves to the car seat. Being ever so careful, we managed to peel ourselves off the seats, forcing us to leave a portion of our dresses behind. Mary had the foresight to bring along our real clothes. She grabbed the bag and we gingerly exited the car.

The stitching began to unravel, and chunks of brightly colored paper flapped against our backsides. Only the front of our dresses remained intact. We took baby steps and stayed at a discrete distance, laughing, and trying our best to keep everything from completely disintegrating. The colorful paper dresses were a hit with everyone in our front-only fashion show. We cautiously backed ourselves up the steps and into the house for a wardrobe change.

The quest for comfort during those close, hot, humid days of July and August didn't abate. Table fans appeared, trips to the beach were embraced, as well as sitting in the shade on the front porch swing, or occasionally on a Sunday evening enjoying ice cream from the New England Dairy, a short walk away. Almost any diversion would do.

In the evening we welcomed the brilliant, fiery orange sun, mercifully descending in the west and wished that maybe, just maybe, we might feel a cooling breeze coming in off Narragansett Bay.

Sunset over Narragansett Bay
Photo: Peggy Haggerty

Family

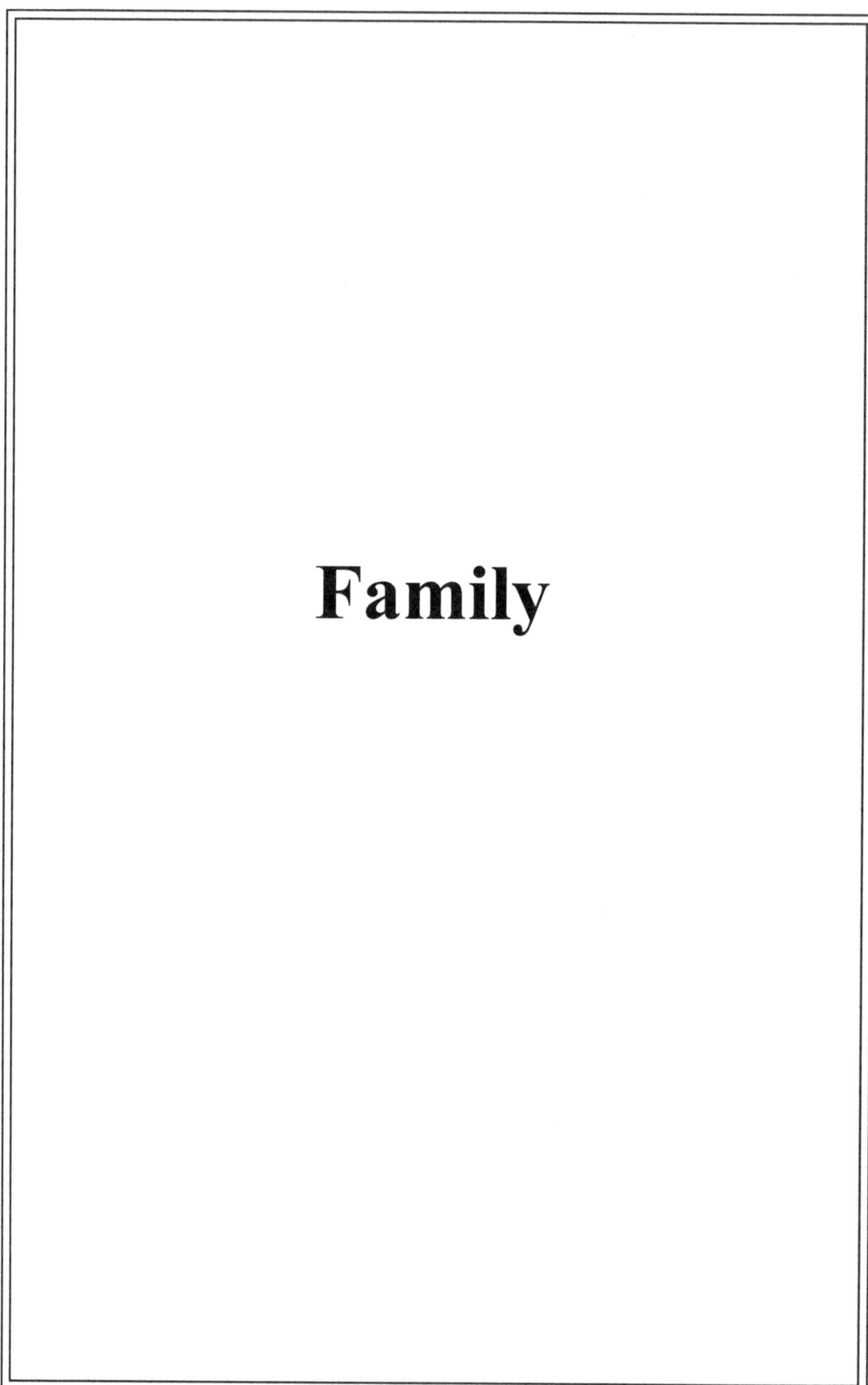

TIES

Good Fortune

Even as a child I recall thinking how lucky I was to be surrounded by a loving family. There were only a few children in this group of adults and we were showered with attention.

My mother's side of the family, the Maguires, had six children born to Catherine Lynch and John Simon Maguire. My Uncle Ed was the oldest and only boy (1889-1960). Next in line of succession, Aunt Anna (1891-1947); then Aunt Es, the third child (1893-1987); Aunt Alice (1896-1986); with Aunt Kay arriving a few years later (1898-1994); and finally the youngest, my mother, Ronnie, short for Veronica (1902-1972).

The Maguire sisters, 1918
Top (l-r): Anna, Esther   Bottom (l-r): Katherine, Veronica, Alice

Ed, Anna, and Esther remained single, living their entire lives in the family home at 49 Dalton Street, Rumford, Rhode Island, with the exception of Esther who later moved to an apartment. The other siblings married late in life; Kay (Bill), and Ronnie (Leo) married in their thirties and Alice (Con, short for Constant) in her forties.

Ronnie and Leo

Ronnie, about age 9

My mother, Ronnie, said as a child she often felt lonesome. She was four years younger than her next sibling. Aunt Anna and Aunt Es were best friends as were Aunt Alice and Aunt Kay, but my mother did find a close friend in her father, called Pa by all his children. She shadowed Pa like a friendly puppy. At lunchtime young Ronnie walked home from Union Primary elementary school for her noon meal. When she finished eating, she fetched the tin lunch pail my grandmother had prepared for my grandfather. My mother walked a mile to deliver it to Pa who worked at the ironworks in the next town, Phillipsdale. My grandfather had the responsible job of foreman. He proudly told my mother that none of the men under his charge had ever had an accident. One of his duties was to watch and instruct the ironworkers on the safest way to toss a red-hot rivet across the room to a man with a bucket poised in readiness to catch the glowing bolt. His youngest child arrived at his workplace five days a week and happily presented him with his sizable lunch.

My mother, like the rest of her family, attended the local public schools and graduated from East Providence High School. She went on to train as a secretary and worked at several jobs requiring the skills she had learned. She was accomplished in shorthand and took pride in the speed at which she could type. She was a competent typist all her life, but never worked outside the home once she married.

My mother was introduced to my father by her best friend, Rena Townsend, in 1932. After a three-year courtship my father, Leo, and my mother, Ronnie, decided to get married. The plan was to have a winter wedding. My mother purchased a handsome array of stylish winter outfits bit-by-bit on her limited secretarial salary for the anticipated honeymoon.

One Saturday afternoon my father arrived at 49 Dalton Street with the news that the wedding date needed to be changed due to a job he had coming up in North Carolina. They would have to get married in early September and head to Ashville immediately following. The south, hot and humid in early fall, meant purchasing new, summer-like clothes. There was little money left to buy a completely different honeymoon trousseau. My mother said she did not want to adjust to any new plans and promptly called off the wedding.

My father didn't attempt to change her mind, but just said he was

Leo and Ronnie having a good time on their honeymoon

Ronnie wearing a new honeymoon outfit

leaving to drive into Providence to get a haircut.

Assessing what she had just done, my mother quickly called a cab and headed into downtown Providence. She knew where my father always had his hair cut and arrived just as the barber was finishing up with his loyal client. My father turned to see a smiling Ronnie coming through the doorway and he knew that the wedding was back on. They were married at St. Margaret's Church in Rumford, Rhode Island, on September 2, 1935, and headed out that evening for Ashville, North Carolina.

They purchased a home in Riverside, Rhode Island. Their three daughters were raised in the buttercup yellow arts and crafts bungalow on Hoppin Avenue. My parents lived in their comfortable three-bedroom home their entire married lives.

My mother was happy being only several miles from her family. She did not have the wanderlust like her sisters, Esther, Alice, and Kay. She was content to stay put.

My father, on the other hand, travelled frequently for his job and was approached at one time by IBM to take an engineering position in Philadelphia. My mother balked at the idea of leaving her sisters and brother in Rumford, so my father declined the offer.

As children, we loved receiving postcards and letters from my father from these seemingly faraway places where he worked designing and supervising the erection of industrial machines.

He had a very different upbringing than my mother experienced. Following his mother's death from tuberculosis in her mid-twenties, he eventually was placed in an orphanage along with his younger

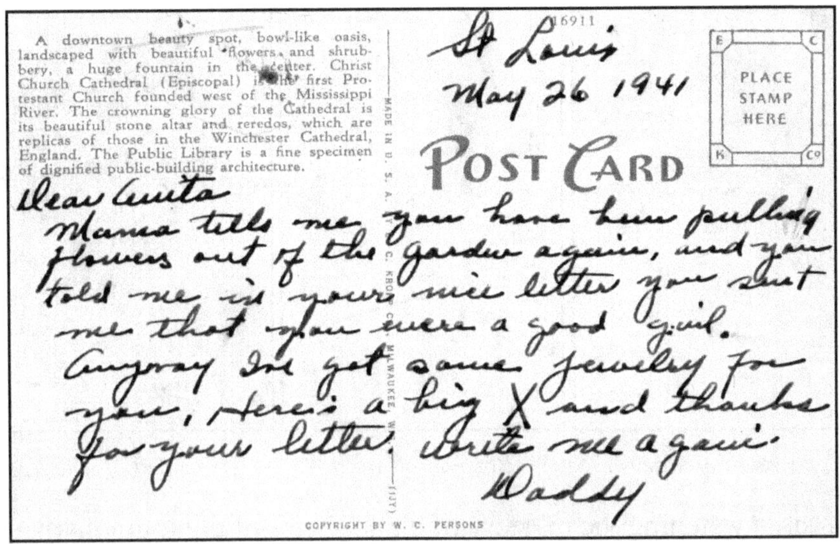

One of the postcards sent to me by my father

brother, Al. They attended school under the strict supervision of the nuns. His education included learning several trades. I remember he told me, much to my surprise, he knew how to make very nice buttonholes for clothing. I am guessing that at one point in his life he learned engineering skills, since that was what he did his entire adult life.

He could have taken the wrong path during those parentless years, but he didn't, nor did my Uncle Al. They both had a knack for always meeting the right people, good people, who cared and nurtured them along the journey.

My father enjoyed photography and his daughters spent many Sunday afternoons sitting for portraits in the studio at one end of the cellar. We sat very still for what seemed to us an eternity on a tall, hard wooden stool under blinding photography lights. He had a darkroom and we all took

My father dressed for work

Portrait of Mary   *Portrait of Anita*   *Portrait of Alicia*

our turns watching the mystery of blank sheets of photography paper gradually change into our portraits. He cautioned us to stand back as he took tongs and submerged the paper in a bath of chemicals. He carefully swished the paper around in the toxic brew as the transformation took place before our eyes. We never tired of observing this magic. My father clipped the photographs on a little clothesline and, when completely dry, we put our newly minted photographs into the enlarger, mostly having fun making ourselves big and then very small with the turn of a dial.

Growing up, dinners at our house took place at the kitchen table beginning about five-thirty or sometimes six, but on Sundays, dinner was at one o'clock. We often ate this meal in the dining room. The kitchen table was covered with a starched tablecloth with a plant or bouquet of flowers in the center to emphasize the importance my mother placed on our daily meal.

We always had dessert. Sometimes fruit was served, but on most occasions it was cake sporting intriguing names: dump cake, poor man's fruit cake; the richer three-egg cake, or the no-egg cake; lightening cake; take-it-easy cake; never-fail cake; daffodil cake; feather cake; and my dad's favorite, hot-milk cake with jam. This was usually in the oven cooking while we ate so it could be served warm the way my father liked it.

Desserts served not as frequently might be snow pudding, blueberry grunt or slump, huckleberry or apple pie, always with a slice of cheddar cheese on top. My mother used to say, "Apple pie without cheese is like a hug without a squeeze." Prune whip was a favorite, but not the dreaded eggy, strange looking floating island. Topping the list of all foods made by mother and enjoyed by her family, especially her three daughters, was the warm oatmeal-molasses bread waiting for us on the wooden cutting board when we arrived home from school.

My mother and father enjoyed taking the family on short trips to New Hampshire or the long ride to Stonington, Maine, for a visit with the Murphys. I am sure my father would have gone on any trip my mother requested, but she was content to stay in and around familiar New England. They saw to it that all three of us attended sleep-over Girl Scout camp for a two-week session most summers when we were young. My mother talked of going to Ireland, but it never materialized. Maybe if she had lived longer, she would have had the opportunity to visit the ancestral homeland of the Maguires, Lynches, and the Cosgroves.

Both my mother and father died following brief illnesses at seventy years of age; my father predeceased my mother by seven years.

My mother's cousin, Eva Reilly, at age 90, wrote the following poem in honor of my mother in December 1972.

For Veronica

The Christmas chimes are ringing
We go to church to pray
While a weary woman's waiting
Growing weaker day by day.

The hands that toiled for others
Are folded on her breast
The feet that carried her to church
Are quietly at rest.

Portrait of Ronnie taken by Leo

Uncle Ed

Uncle Ed, my godfather, was a bit of a character and somewhat mysterious, but his young nieces and nephews loved being in his company, mostly because he enjoyed having us around and laughed at our antics, no matter what we were up to or how badly we behaved.

He was of medium height with sparse, thin, steel-grey hair and a neatly groomed comb-over that rose straight up

Uncle Ed, 1896

from his scalp on a windy day. When this occurred, he just patted it back down and went about his business.

On Sundays Uncle Ed always wore a three-piece suit, mostly wool, that I am sure Aunt Esther chose for him with her discount at The Outlet Company. You would think wearing a vest provided the perfect concealer for his pot belly, but no, it only accentuated this persistent protrusion.

I am sure he never missed Sunday Mass at St. Margaret's Church. He said the rosary often, but I do not know if it was a daily practice. He liked to relax on one of the two rocking chairs in the kitchen and at times I saw him fingering his rosary beads. My uncle did not want anyone to know he was praying, so he quietly slipped his rosary and the slender accompanying missal to the far end of the windowsill when anyone entered the room.

I never saw him have a single alcoholic drink. Back then the Catholic Church, at the time of confirmation, encouraged boys to take "The Pledge." It was a common practice in those days for these young people to promise to abstain from alcohol for life. I do recall him buying cider in the fall and letting it sit, unopened, in the pantry nestled next to the wood box for a considerable amount of time.

Uncle Ed joined the Rhode Island State Guard, the forerunner of the National Guard, for three years. Having been trained as a machinist in the service he went on to work at Herreshoff Marine in Bristol and he was later employed by the Torpedo Station in Newport.

As a machinist Uncle Ed had a very interesting cellar. Lots of tiny yet surprisingly heavy tools were in drawers, on hooks, or lying about on his workbench. At times I examined them but did not ask to use these strangely shaped instruments. They were nothing like the normal tools in my dad's basement workshop.

In the very center of the cellar, a huge stone wheel attached to a wooden frame proved to be an intriguing piece of equipment. My sister, Mary, and I (as well as our cousins, Tom and Mike, if they happened to be visiting) would watch the wheel rotate at a modified and calculated speed as Uncle Ed's foot pushed down on the wooden peddle, sharpening one of Aunt Esther's kitchen knives, all the while pressing the knife against the stone. We stood back, mesmerized, as sparks flew in every direction. We wanted to tell Uncle Ed to be careful or one of those sparks could catch the house on fire, but it never did.

As soon as he vacated the basement, Mary, Tom, Mike, and I took turns forcing the peddle down with all our strength, hard and fast. The peddle was connected to cables attached to the circular stone and caused the wheel to rotate at a dizzying speed. It was difficult to slow down, especially if we heard footsteps descending the cellar stairs.

As a longtime member of the National Geographic Society, Uncle Ed enjoyed learning about exotic destinations around the world, places he would only get to see on the pages of the *National Geographic* magazines that he piled one on top of another in his second-floor bedroom, never to be tossed out. He read history, studied maps, and found geography fascinating.

I remember seeing my cousin Tom and Uncle Ed sitting in the kitchen at my grandmother's, heads close together, discussing something. Tom said they liked to talk about serious subjects like history or the Navy, but what he remembered most was that Uncle Ed visited his house after Mass every Sunday.

"Mum read *The New York Times* on Sunday, in fact the three of us read it. He instructed me to take note of who had written the article, think about what was being said, ask myself why this topic was being examined, and to form my own opinions," Tom said.

Tom went on to tell me that he never thought too much about these lessons at the time, but as he grew older, he realized Uncle Ed not only gave him a life-long love of reading but taught him to read critically.

Uncle Ed, age 43

Uncle Ed loved his car and drove it at top speed, only braking at a stop sign within a foot or two of its appearance along the side of the road. This sudden braking caused all his passengers to fly forward. His idea of driving was to go from point A to point B without ever stopping.

When Rumford began to install additional traffic signals throughout the town I remember him saying, "Those lights are going to cause nothing but trouble." His passengers were grateful to have the new street signals make an appearance at busy intersections.

Sometimes on a Sunday when my father worked out of town, Uncle Ed would pick Mary and me up for a visit to Dalton Street. I know my mother prayed for our safe delivery, but the return trip for that seven-mile drive home to Riverside worried her more with night approaching. My mother told us she usually had just completed saying the rosary as his car headlights illuminated our driveway. My sisters and I were always scared being in the car with my uncle at the wheel, but we never had an accident when we drove with him, nor do I think he was ever involved in one.

He built a gas-driven lawn mower long before you could purchase one at the hardware store. We enjoyed sitting, just out of harm's way, watching him cut the grass. Uncle Ed never got the motor to adjust properly. He ran around the yard holding on to the wooden handle for dear life with his homemade contraption charging forward at a three-mile-an-hour clip.

My Uncle Ed and Aunt Es came to Sunday dinner at our house the week before Thanksgiving in November of 1960. As they were leaving, they both gave us their usual goodbye hug. Uncle Ed walked through the pantry, got to the back door and turned around. He came over to me and gave me a crushing second hug. This had never happened before.

The following Saturday he attended his best friend John Keene's daughter's wedding at The Neighborhood Club in Quincy, just south of Boston. Upon leaving the reception, he started to walk to his car for the ride back to Rumford. He never got there. My uncle collapsed suddenly onto the sidewalk and died of a heart attack.

I had been in Boston with my future husband, Bill, on that November day. I arrived home late, entered the mostly darkened house and went upstairs for the night. The following morning, I walked into the kitchen. My father was waiting for me.

"I have some sad news, Anita. Your Uncle Ed died yesterday afternoon."

"Dad, why didn't you tell me when I got in last night?"

"No, Anita, bad news can always wait for the morning."

I never forgot what my dad said to me and I have practiced his advice when called for over the years.

Following Uncle Ed's death, my aunt gave my cousin, Michael, his old grey car that always had a hole in the floor on the front passenger side.

Michael said to me not long ago, "I don't know why but I could not get that car of Uncle Ed's to ever run again."

Uncle Ed's death left a huge void in all our lives and he was the first Maguire not to be waked from the front parlor of the Maguire home on Dalton Street. He was laid out in Providence, at Monahan & Sons Funeral Home, and in time, with other relatives to follow his lead, my mother being the exception. She announced more than once,

"Just wake me at the Watson Funeral Home. I believe they can use the business."

Aunt Kay and Uncle Bill

Aunt Kay, the fifth in line of the six siblings, appeared as thin as a rail, or skinny as a bean pole, but I thought of her as being very stylish. She wore mostly black clothing accentuated with tan or white accessories. Her hair, a variety of earth tones, cascaded down her back. By day she styled it caught in combs at the back of her head, but when readying for bed, after having donned an unadulterated white to-the-floor cotton nightshirt, she wove it into a single loose braid, looking not unlike a heroine from the pages of a Jane Austen novel.

My cousin Tom recently reminded me that she was the only woman around town who wore slacks.

"All women wore dresses in those days, but not Mum," he said.

Her slacks were loose and tailored, exuding a hint of elegance and grace.

My mother said she remembered her older sister, Kay, also known as Katherine, as sickly, yet she lived longer than any Maguire. Kay, a bookish child, my mother said, could often be found sitting on the parlor floor reading, with her back to the wall, oblivious to the ever-present company milling about. Her interest in reading and learning continued throughout her life.

Following graduation from high school and Rhode Island Normal School she taught in East Providence. During summer breaks Aunt Kay travelled to New York City to live with her best friend, my Aunt Alice. She enrolled in nearby Columbia University and one day confided in us that her favorite class was dancing. The instructor required the students to leap around the gymnasium all the while keeping a seven-foot long silk piece of fabric from touching the floor. A fellow dancer in her class that summer was Georgia O'Keeffe.

She attended Brown University at night following a day of teaching. We questioned if she did get a degree from Brown since, at that time, the university enrolled only males. With her original diploma in hand I called the archival library at Brown. The woman on the other end of the telephone paused only a few minutes before she said,

"Yes, Catherine (Catherinam) Winifred (Winifredam) Maguire indeed graduated from Brown University, class of 1930."

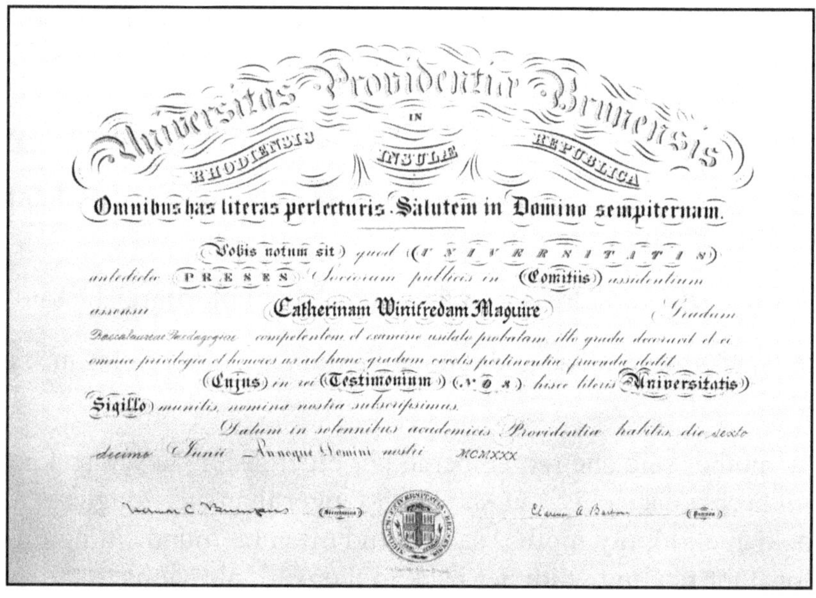

Catherine's diploma from Brown University

If Aunt Kay had her way I am sure her diploma would have read Katherine, not Catherine, since she used many creative spellings of her name during her lifetime, always beginning with a K, but never with a C.

I believe that going to school nights, not days, made her a registered student in this male bastion. I think that if she attended as a daytime undergraduate, her degree would have been awarded by Pembroke, the female division of the college.

Picture of my mom, age 25, wearing the Tree of Life pin that was designed and made by Aunt Kay

She found time to attend Rhode Island School of Design and became an accomplished silversmith. My sister, Alicia, has the sterling flatware Aunt Kay designed, and I have a handsome circular Tree of Life pin. Mary, her godchild, received a four-piece hammered sterling coffee set. I remember my aunt saying that it was not uncommon for designers from Gorham Sterling, whose headquarters were in Providence, to walk into their classrooms and take note of the students' designs.

As I now reflect on what she achieved as a young woman I am amazed, but growing up I did not think it out of the ordinary. She was just Aunt Kay to me.

In July of 1935 she married a town policeman, William Reynolds. I don't know where they met, but my gregarious uncle was a good match for my serious, studious, organized aunt. They had one child, Alice, who died of leukemia in the spring of 1941.

Not long after Alice's death, my Aunt Alice, a volunteer at the New York (city) Foundling Home, told my aunt Kay and Uncle Bill there were two young brothers up for adoption and she wondered if they would be interested. They were, and on December 19, 1942, three-year-old Michael and five-year-old Tommy came to live in Rumford. We were happy to welcome our new cousins.

Kay and Bill's wedding, July 1935
l-r: My Dad (Leo), My Mom (Ronnie), Kay, and Bill

Recently, I asked Michael and Tom if they remembered anything at all from that period of their lives. Michael said he remembered a crack in the ceiling over his crib in the orphanage. Tom replied that he had no memory of anything at all except the train ride from New York to Providence.

Michael and Tom's adoption made no difference in how they were treated in our family. They were our cousins and all the aunts and uncles were theirs too. We were all on equal footing.

Aunt Kay and Uncle Bill purchased one of the oldest houses in Rumford for their family of four. It was built originally for the chaplain who ministered to the men constructing the railroad in that part of Rhode Island. The house's ramshackle appearance did not resemble any place you would want to live, but they rebuilt it into an attractive home.

The empty lot alongside the house proved to be the ideal spot for Aunt Kay to garden. Each spring, after the boys were older, they

Mary and me with Tom and Mike, our new cousins

readied the soil by turning over the substantial plot of land shovel-full by shovel-full. The bounty of vegetables and flowers was shared among family and neighbors. She avoided using chemicals in her gardening, but nourished the soil and kept the weeds in check by applying decomposed grass clippings. Aunt Kay recorded her progress in a meticulous planting diary and each year incorporated a new unfamiliar vegetable to plant. As the years went by, to unburden some of her outdoor workload, she began to grass-in narrow strips of her once sizable garden.

My aunt and uncle loved the water and the four of them often drove to the coast of Maine to visit my Aunt Alice and Uncle Con. They enjoyed exploring the miles of sandy beaches in South County, Rhode Island, and along the picturesque shores and often rocky coastline of the East Bay area. Uncle Bill fished while my aunt looked for unusual shells or dug for clams.

One time she said to me, "I don't know why we never bought a boat. We enjoyed the beach so much. We just didn't think of it I guess."

I loved to unexpectedly spot my uncle riding down the road in his very official looking police uniform astride a police motorcycle. He wore knee-high thick leather puttees to protect his legs from injury and sizable suede gloves as a safeguard for his hands. I gave him a big wave and received a broad grin in return, but during this brief, friendly encounter he never took his hands off the massive handlebars.

Following Uncle Bill's retirement, he enjoyed antiquing with my aunt. He could never resist searching out silly toys. When we visited he always demonstrated a newly discovered treasure. Sometimes it was a clown flipping in never-ending summersaults or a toy car that drove erratically over the floor crashing into walls. It was fun to watch him as he wound the side key of a toy and laughed at the antics of his latest juvenile curio.

Aunt Kay continued to teach school on a limited basis and taught piano to a few students. This gave her time to pursue a favorite hobby, rug hooking. Her huge wooden hooking frame, a permanent fixture in the living room adjacent to the fireplace, always had a rug

Hooked rug made by Kay in the 1940s,
adapted from a Blue Willow china design

in progress. An antique basket filled with rolled balls of colorful, cut wool strips used in constructing loops to create a rug, resembled a striking contemporary art installation. She designed and hooked rugs for every room in their house. The extensive living room rug, made up of numerous twelve-inch squares, was created to represent whatever was taking place at that time, be it an anniversary, holiday, or a family event.

Aunt Kay lived twenty-four years following the death of my Uncle Bill at the age of seventy one in 1970. She sent us a letter at Christmas time expressing her life without Bill,

"It is snowing out now and very lonely. But I know it is better this way. I had hoped to be the one to go first. I just accept the loneliness as part of God's will. Good night my dear ones. Aunt Kay."

A year later, after the passing of Uncle Con, my Aunt Alice sold their Maine home and moved in with her sister, Kay, for nine years. Kay continued to reside at her Ferris Avenue home in Rumford, with her faithful shaggy, black Schnauzer, Sam, until two years before her death in 1994 at the age of ninety six.

Alice and her life-long friend and younger sister, Katherine, 1899

Kay and Alice

Aunt Alice and Uncle Con

They were the love couple in our family. My uncle Con adored my Aunt Alice and the feeling was mutual. She could do no wrong in my uncle's eyes.

"My Alice, isn't she something?"

This compliment was heard many times by all those within earshot and it always made us smile. We never tired of hearing it.

In the Maguire clan, Aunt Alice came as close as you could get to a middle child in a family of six. All her life she remained independent, willful, funny, full of surprises, and, like her brother and sisters, devout.

Aunt Alice attended Union Primary Elementary School (built 1873), then went on to East Providence High School. She graduated from Bryant & Stratton, receiving training as a secretary. With her newly earned diploma, this pretty, dark-haired beauty of the family, soon departed the safe enclave of Rumford for the hustle and bustle of New York City in search of employment and adventure.

Alice, high school graduation

Aunt Alice found housing, along with many other young women of that era, in an all-female hotel, I believe the Barbizon. There she met Barbara, a young woman from England. The two became life-long friends, and after they each married, the couples lived in the same apartment complex for many years and later they all retired to Deer Isle, Maine.

An early memory I have of my aunt is seeing her stepping out of a car at my grandmother's after having been picked up at the Union train station in Providence. Her sisters rushed out to the driveway to greet her. I stood back, enraptured by her flaming red hair. I did not

Aunt Alice on a visit home from NYC in 1939
holding her nieces (l-r), Mary, me, and Baby Alice

know anyone in the world who had that vivid color. I peppered my mother with questions. She explained that Aunt Alice was not born with that unnatural shade, but dyed it with something called a henna rinse. The style-conscious Maguire women must have registered their disapproval because she did not visit again with that intense color of red hair.

My uncle met my aunt, I believe, through their mutual friends, the Johnstons, Barbara and Matt. Constant Stewart Murphy, always called Con, originally came from Maine. He maintained the family home, situated high on the rugged, rocky coast on a stretch of land called Greenhead on Deer Isle until his death. My uncle travelled the world many times over with his job as an engineer on various ocean-going vessels.

Alice and Con were married in New York City on July 3, 1943. He was not a Catholic and this did not sit well with the church or my aunt. It was referred to as a mixed marriage, but that did not keep the immediate family from attending the ceremony. I can remember my mother having her picture taken in our driveway, looking stylish and very un-Riverside, before heading to New York city for the wedding.

Aunt Alice wanted Con to join forces with the Maguires and convert to Catholicism. As young children, my sister, Mary, and I said our prayers each night on our knees beside our beds, reciting our devotions. At the very end we could be heard to say aloud,

"Please give us world peace. Help Uncle Con to stop drinking and please help him become a Catholic."

I had never seen Uncle Con drink, but he must have if we were praying for him. A few years following their marriage, I am sure under unrelenting persuasion by my headstrong aunt, he began religious instruction and converted to Catholicism. Now a "devout Catholic" he practiced his new-found faith all his life and never wavered from the many rules of the church. I heard later that he stopped drinking.

Not long after his conversion my aunt and uncle took a walk in Central Park. As they stood on a bridge overlooking a stream, Aunt Alice asked Con if she could look at his ruby-and-diamond-studded Mason ring. He took it off his finger and handed it to her. With one quick toss she threw it over the railing. It splashed on the water's surface and quickly disappeared into the murky, wet quagmire below.

"Oh, Alice, my ring!"

"Now, Con, you can no longer be a Mason. You are a Catholic now."

The tale goes that my uncle never did get angry at his beloved Alice. There were no hard feelings. They hopped on the subway and returned to their apartment on 125th street.

All members of our family visited the city dwellers as often as their schedules would allow. Mary and I travelled by train to New York for a week-long stay when I was nine and Mary ten and a half. We joined them in their tiny, fifth-floor apartment.

Each day our vacation began with a hearty breakfast and later a robust and filling lunch that never varied: always thick, difficult-to-digest, Velveeta cheese sandwiches. Aunt Alice felt an obligation to feed us nutritiously. She had read an advertisement that lauded Velveeta as being packed with protein and good for growing bodies. We dutifully ate our cheesy lunches every day.

Alice and Con, 1962

The apartment kitchen window, often wide open during a particularly warm July, was only several feet away from another building whose windows remained up most of the day. We could hear a piano playing, sometimes horns, but most often someone singing.

"Now, girls, if that music bothers you, just let me know and I will shut the window," exclaimed my aunt on several occasions.

The music we were "subjected to" was from the rising stars rehearsing at the world-famous Julliard School of Music.

There was adventure on every corner. On our initial excursion, via a double-decker bus, we paid a visit to Grant's tomb. This attraction did seem a strange place for her to bring us since we did not know who General Grant was, but my aunt thought that any exposure to American history would be good for her two nieces.

We took the Staten Island ferry over and back for a nickel, and the following day peered at New Jersey and beyond from the top of the Empire State Building. The best day ever had to be the Coney Island trip. I remember Steeplechase Park and seeing the oversized image of the smiling man at the entrance, with an abundance of very white, rounded teeth and an abnormally wide smile. We climbed to the top of a huge polished wooden slide, gripping a pillow to sit on, and flew down the steep passageway. We landed in a circular bowl, causing us to twirl around and around just to the verge of getting ill.

The agenda included a trip to see the mummified body of the first American saint, Mother Cabrini. The shrine, a long bus ride to northern Manhattan, resulted in me getting bus sick and the three of us having to vacate and trudge the remainder of the way on foot. Mary and I stared, without a word, at Mother Cabrini's body, encased in a glass coffin-like enclosure. Clad in her nun's habit, she appeared long, thin, and flat as a pancake. I learned later that her head was missing and on display somewhere in Italy. A wax facsimile sufficed in place of the real thing. Had Mary and I been aware of this oddity I know we would have leaned further over the altar railing to get a better look.

We explored the streets of the garment district and gazed in windows full of hats and accessories. I spotted a drunk man lying in the gutter thrashing about. I pointed at him and laughed. My aunt came to an abrupt halt in the empty street, took hold of my arm, and turned me around to face her.

"Anita, when you see someone who is different from you and especially if the person has troubles, you see it once."

She did not elaborate beyond that simple directive. She took my hand and we continued crossing the street. I knew what my aunt was conveying even though I was just nine years old.

We enjoyed many good times with my aunt and uncle long after they moved from 125th and on to another, larger, apartment in Fort Lee, New Jersey, in the shadow of the George Washington Bridge, and later to Deer Isle in the town of Stonington, Maine. More good times than I can count continued over the years. Aunt Alice was so much fun.

Trips to Maine included lobster, clams, picnics on the rocks down by the water's edge, and hiking in the cool pine woods. I recall sitting on their wrap-around porch gazing out on the scattering of small islands and further out, a larger island, Isle au Haut, and a branch of Acadia National Park. Beyond these dots, tall pines and craggy rock formations, the blue Atlantic stretched out to the horizon. This breathtaking panorama remains a lasting memory.

Views from Alice and Con's window in Maine

One early spring day in 1971 my mother called me when my family was living in Baltimore to tell me Uncle Con had some serious health issues. I could not imagine that loving couple being separated by death. I flew to Maine alone, leaving my husband, Bill, in charge of our four young children, knowing that it may be the last time I would see my dear uncle.

We didn't do much that long weekend but walk through the dense woods along the path of soft pine needles leading down to the water's edge, eat hearty meals, and talk.

There was a knock on my bedroom door one morning. It was Uncle Con.

"Anita, come to our bedroom. I have something to show you."

I put on my robe and went to the end of the hall to their room: a beautiful spot, with the windows framing the ocean view.

Aunt Alice had only been awake a short time. She looked at me and smiled,

"Good morning, Anita, my dear."

37

Uncle Con walked to the side of their bed, reached over and lovingly put his hand against my aunt's pale pink cheek. He hesitated a moment then in a soft voice, almost a whisper said,

"Anita, my Alice, isn't she something?"

1954 family gathering. Top (l-r): Family friend, Michael Reynolds, Uncle Bill
Middle: My sister Mary, Aunt Kay, Aunt Es, and me
Front: My Mother Ronnie, Uncle Con holding my sister Alicia, Aunt Alice,
Tommy Reynolds

CATHERINE LYNCH MAGUIRE

Momma/Grandma

Grandma appeared frail as she lay propped up on her brown, metal hospital bed. Her fluffy, snow-white hair was held in place atop her head by two oversized, tortoise-shell hair pins. A black eye patch covered the depression where a diseased right eye once had been.

Grandma's head turned toward me as I entered the room. Her good eye widened watching her young granddaughter approach carrying her lunch. "Hi, Grandma, Aunt Es said I could feed you your soup."

I held in my hand a small, flower-decorated, porcelain container that closely resembled Aladdin's magical lamp: a handle on one end and a long pouring spout on the other. It contained barely warm, homemade beef broth.

I adjusted the pillow and tucked a large, white, cloth napkin under her chin. "Grandma, open your mouth so I can pour it down."

Those words, coming from a little girl who could only reach her by standing on the blue painted step stool, must have been frightening to someone helpless in bed.

Grandma's clamped-shut mouth did not dissuade me. I kept up a steady stream of chatter about Aunt Es's good-tasting soup. In time she opened her mouth. Her lips pursed just wide enough for me to insert the pouring device. I tipped the strange looking container and she took a swallow. She closed her good eye and continued to drink the clear consommé.

Grandma fell asleep before I completed my task. The broth began to roll down the sides of her mouth and on to the pillow. I grabbed the cotton napkin and tried my best to clean up the spilled soup.

"Aunt Es, I think Grandma is finished."

As messy as it was, I liked playing nurse. This privilege of feeding my grandmother, entrusted to me by my aunt, was never extended to my sister or my two cousins, but maybe they never asked.

Sometimes Grandma treated our cousins, Mike and Tom, and my sister, Mary, and me. She directed us to open the top, right-hand drawer in her dresser and take out her black, pigskin pocketbook and open the small change purse inside. She told us each to take a quarter. In the standard of the mid-1940s, this represented a lot of money to four young children.

My mother told me that Grandma had been an excellent seamstress and ran a small dressmaking business from her home for many years. Her clients were several wealthy women living on the East Side. This area of Providence, at the top of College Hill, adjacent to Brown University, is an area of grand homes even today. These women would come for fittings and my mother said it was not unusual for one or two to drop by on a Sunday and stay for dinner. The guests were served first and received the best cuts of meat, then the plate would be passed to my grandfather, grandmother, and the children in ranking of their age. My mother said there was not much left on the platter by the time it reached her.

My grandmother made beautiful clothes for her daughters. I have the heavy, tan, linen, driving coat she made for Aunt Kay and a few other outfits. My sister Alicia's wedding dress, a delicate detailed, white cotton batiste gown, was originally Aunt Esther's ankle-length high school graduation ensemble sewed by my grandmother.

I never remember my grandmother, Catherine Lynch Maguire, being in good health. The lovely old white clapboard Victorian home with shutters the color of shamrocks was built, in part, by my grandfather, John Simon Maguire, in the late 1800s. They were married at St. Margaret's Church in Rumford, Rhode Island, in June of 1889.

Their six children (Edward Louis, Anna Loretta, Mary Esther, Alice Genevieve, Catherine Winifred, and Maria Veronica were all born

John Simon Maguire   *Catherine Lynch Maguire*

at home with the exception of my mother. She went by Veronica, Ronnie, or Ron all her life.

Being the youngest, my mother told me she got to go places with Grandma. She said that one time a horse and buggy drew up to the front of the house. Having no one to leave her youngest child with my mother accompanied Grandma to a funeral. The inside of the carriage, Mother said, was warm and toasty because hot coals in a metal container under their seat kept the carriage comfortable on a biting cold winter day.

Aunt Kay remembered her mother telling her that the Lynch side of the family came from County Claire, Ireland, early in the Irish migration, probably during the potato famine. Some members of the family landed in Canada and others in Rhode Island. Aunt Kay said, "On occasion Momma travelled to Sherrington, a short distance north of the New York state border, to visit her Canadian relatives."

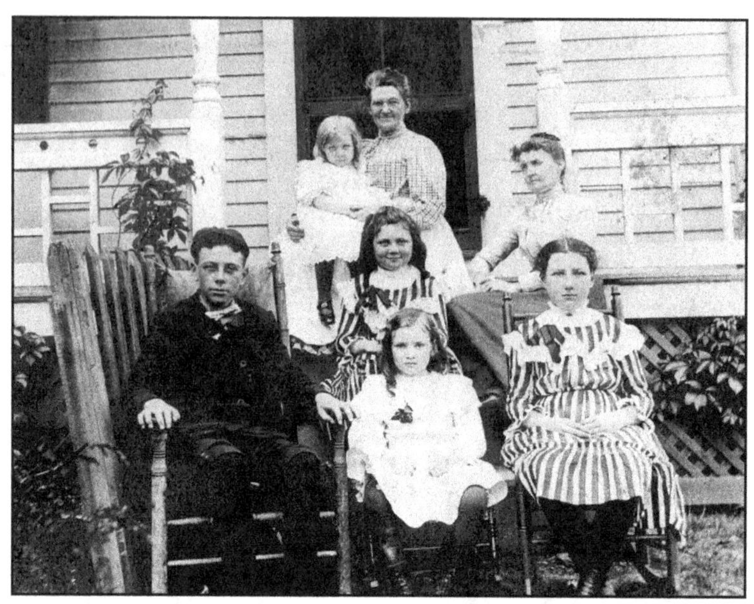

Family sitting on steps at Dalton Street house, 1902
Top: Grandma holding Catherine
Middle: Ed, Esther, and "Auntie" (a relative who helped care for the children)
Front: Alice, Anna

Aunt Kay thought of her mother as a pioneer woman of sorts. She told her daughter, Kay, that she once borrowed her father's horse and sleigh and drove alone to Putman, Connecticut, to attend a funeral, a distance of over twenty-five miles. She stopped often on that wintery journey to wipe snow off of road markers to guide her along the way. She reached her destination on time and arrived back home unscathed.

My grandmother, Catherine, also known as Kate, was brought up on a farm at the foot of Dalton Street in Rumford where her parents, Catherine Cosgrove and John Lynch, farmed their small piece of property. When my grandmother and grandfather were about to be married, Grandma purchased a sizable plot of land situated at the very top of the hill on Dalton Street at auction for a few dollars.

My grandfather's family, the Maguires, can trace their surname back to County Fermanagh, Ireland, though my mother believed some may have settled further south in Roscommon. The Maguires ruled Fermanagh and were the dominant society from the thirteenth to the seventeenth centuries. They were the kings of Fermanagh. The Maguire clan motto is "Justice and Fortitude Are Invincible."

This embroidary depicts Great-Grandpa Maguire's farm house and barn on Bourne Ave in Rumford, RI. It was made by his nephew, Willie Obert, of Erie, PA, who was recovering from an illness and spent time with the Maguires as a teenager.

John Maguire lived a short distance from Catherine on Bourne Avenue on several acres of land that they farmed in Rumford. His father came from Ireland to manage the imposing Howard farm in Cranston, Rhode Island, which is now the Rhode Island Department of Corrections. At one time a psychiatric hospital, simply known as Howard, shared this acreage.

In a letter to my oldest son, Aunt Kay wrote that "Pa, as a very young man, drove a team of horses with a heavy scoop attached in the rear to dig cellars for the houses near the Rumford Chemical

Works. The Yankees stoned his horses and him because he was Irish. The Irish were hardy. They were poets, artists, and fighters."

My mother often remembered coming home from school and finding my grandmother resting with her head down, whispering to her youngest child, "Veronica, please start the potatoes for dinner." Grandma suffered from migraines. This probably resulted from the stress of having babies in her thirties and my mother being born in my grandma's mid-forties.

Before Grandma became bed-ridden, she enjoyed sitting in the wooden lounge chair on the front porch overlooking Omega Pond located at the bottom of the hill. Mary and I often joined her but were never tempted to run to the pond when she dozed off. Scary stories that a few children had drowned in that body of water were not folklore. I don't remember what we talked about with Grandma, but we liked being there with her.

Grandma died at home on June 17, 1945, in her 89th year. Her wake was in the front parlor of her home. She spent her entire life on Dalton Street in the then rural town of Rumford, Rhode Island.

The funeral was arranged by Monahan's in Providence. Thomas Monahan, who once ran the company with his son, was a longtime family friend and former unsuccessful suitor of my grandmother.

Out of curiosity, I recently searched for Monahan's on the internet. Indeed, it is still in operation. The stately, old, white-columned East Side mansion, now over 125 years old, had a few additional owners over the years. In grandmother's and my mother's time, it was T.F. Monahan & Son, Undertakers.

I read some startling information in the ad: "Funeral Home Opens Irish Pub: seating for 50. Monahan's will soon serve beer, wine, liquor, and food on the lower level of the funeral home, in addition to carrying on its usual function on the first floor."

I could not imagine my family hiring T. F. Monahan to do the funeral arrangements for anyone who lived at 49 Dalton Street if liquor was served at their place of business. My grandmother's home had only one bottle of spirits. A dusty bottle of wine lingered on the very top shelf of the pantry. When I inquired about the wine, my aunt replied, "Oh, it is there just in case a priest stops by!"

I wondered why a priest would need a glass of wine when no one else ever had any. I didn't understand her response but did not inquire further.

I could almost hear my mother and aunts reacting to the stunning news that Monahan's had now acquired a liquor license for the proud, sedate, long-standing Providence, Rhode Island, undertaking establishment. "Glory be to Gawd, if Momma knew Monahan's was serving liquor she would just roll over in her grave."

John and Kate

THE FUNERAL FEAST

Anna L. Maguire, RN

Aunt Anna as a young girl

Aunt Anna was dead. She lay in her coffin in my grandmother's dimly lit front parlor: unsmiling, clasping her rosary beads, right hand over left; clothed in her Sunday best. She appeared older than her fifty-six years. Aunt Anna died on January 18, 1947.

I loved my Aunt Anna, especially her extraordinary laugh. She would thrust her head back, then bring it slowly forward emitting glorious, high pitched laughter. I usually did not understand what was going on when my mother and her four sisters gathered in the kitchen all chatting in unison, but her happiness became mine and I in turn smiled.

Illness plagued Aunt Anna as far back as nursing school. She had several serious diseases when attending St. Joseph's Hospital School of Nursing in Providence. School included long days of study and patient care, but another aspect of being a nurse in those days was hard, physical labor. Nurses were required to scrub the tile corridors of the hospital on their hands and knees and were not respected by the doctors or the administration. My mother told me that the treatment of the young nurses was often cruel and harsh. Aunt Anna had pneumonia early on and later typhoid fever. It was whispered that her kidneys were not functioning well. As a young child I thought that being a public health nurse meant her chances of recovering were better than most people. Mother said her sister, Anna, was always ill.

But I remember a period when she was not sick. One summer when Dad was on a job out of town, she invited Mother, Mary, and me to join her on a vacation to East Dennis on Cape Cod.

The drive seemed never ending but, once over the Bourne Bridge, we knew we were close to our destination. Aunt Anna drove along route 6A, and then headed out on the narrow road to East Dennis, a small picturesque town dotted with many weather-beaten, grey clapboard homes.

Anna L. Maguire, RN

She knew exactly where to go and turned into the driveway of an authentic looking log cabin with a large front, screened-in porch that stretched across the entire length of the house. The main attraction happened to be in the front yard. Scattered about the lawn were several brightly painted miniature metal animals, each supported by a heavy coil. Mary and I spent hours hopping from one to another, bouncing as far as the thick spirals would bend.

Many years later while visiting Rhode Island on a trip from my then home outside Philadelphia, we decided to go on an adventure to locate the cabin. My mother, my infant son, Bill, my sister Alicia, and I headed off to The Cape in search of our once-upon-a-time vacation spot. My mother had no trouble finding our special lodging of long ago. To our delight the animals were still there on the lawn and the cabin had a vacancy sign out front. We stayed the night.

"Maybe we'll come back some day when the baby is bigger," I said. Years went by. I became the busy mother of four children and forgot about ever returning.

The Cape was always a favorite vacation spot for my Aunt Es and Aunt Anna. Their trip often involved searching gift and antique shops for items to add to my Aunt Anna's ever-expanding collection of milk glass. The two bosom companions enjoyed many shopping expeditions driving around the quaint, seaside towns.

I never knew Anna to have a boyfriend, but I think she did. I discovered a postcard dated 1920 from Rotterdam. The message read, *From Ned. I wish that you were here.* I also found the photograph that told its own story. I would like to believe that the handsome young man sitting in front of my smiling aunt was her beau, Ned.

Anna with Ned, Ronnie, "Auntie," and a cousin

Sometimes we were lucky enough to be at Dalton Street when my aunt arrived home after work. My sister and I darted across the yard to greet Aunt Anna as we watched her car with its massive curvy fenders and wide running boards climb the gradual driveway incline.

I liked the official way Aunt Anna looked in her tailored, navy blue public health nurse's uniform. Her cap resembled that of a Navy Wave. She carried a large, heavy, black leather bag held shut with a sizable silver lock. We were curious to know the contents, but never asked her to open it for us to examine. Aunt Anna gave us an affectionate hug with her free arm.

My aunt found her time practicing as a public health nurse in and around Rumford to be gratifying and enjoyable. Her kindness, empathy, pleasant manner, and nursing skills were remembered by the families that she served long after her death.

At some point my aunt realized that she could no longer work due to lingering illnesses. My Aunt Esther took on the responsibility of caring for her beloved friend and older sister, Anna. I am not sure how long she was ill. In time she was hospitalized. I can recall standing on the lawn and seeing her waving to us from a third-floor hospital window. Mother told Mary and me to look up. She waved a few times but did not smile. We waved back. I did not express my deep sadness. I wanted to tell my mother, but my throat felt tight and my face hot. I tried not to cry. I knew I would not see my aunt again. Questions about her sickness were not discussed. I never really found out what caused her death.

"God's will," I was told.

A mild, mid-January day greeted us the afternoon of her wake. My Aunt Anna's many friends and relatives arrived at 49 Dalton Street in a steady procession up to the front door.

My sister, Mary, and I took turns greeting the mourners. Each time I opened the weighty front door I glanced at the beautiful purple crepe, not unlike Grandma's, adorned with ribbons and fresh flowers, tied securely to the brass bell pull. Somber-faced men and women, carrying food, spiritual bouquets, and Mass cards, hugged and kissed family members. My mother and my aunts graciously accepted the food and placed it on the long linoleum shelf in the pantry just off the kitchen.

Chocolate brownies, Indian pudding thick with molasses, Boston cream pie, oatmeal raisin cookies, and fruit and nut breads began to fill the panty.

Fudge came with the Finn sisters, Sadie and Margaret. I knew I could count on them for something rich, creamy, and delicious. Their very social bachelor brother, Francis, quickly paid his respects and joined the men in the smoke-filled kitchen where they were drinking cider or Moxie. The Maguire household, even in death, did not serve liquor. Moxie, the beverage of choice, resembled Coca Cola and bubbled in the glass when ice cubes were added, but that was where the similarity ended. Moxie, I thought, had the flavor of what you might imagine to be the taste of crude oil.

Cousin Eva Reilly carried in a plate of sandwiches with the crusts removed. A paper-thin slice of turkey lay in each little sandwich with a meager brushing of mayonnaise. This was not surprising. Eva was always very slim and thrifty.

Agnes Maguire, a first cousin of Aunt Anna, arrived with her usual air of authority. She came through the parlor into the kitchen with one arm as long as the other. In other words, she brought no turkey sandwiches, no sliced ham, not even a pound box of Fanny Farmer chocolates. Agnes gave her nod of approval to the sumptuous spread on the pantry shelf and quickly departed to pay her respects.

Agnes worked her way around the room, introducing herself to those she did not know as if she were running for mayor. Agnes was a maiden lady of short stature, stocky, and the no-nonsense principal of Bourne Avenue School built on property that at one time had been my great-grandfather's farm. Agnes, the rich relative, and the last of the Maguire/McKenna line, had three large, terrifying Doberman Pinchers, an attractive, white, old-fashioned rambling farmhouse, and a fancy, dark blue, two-seater coupe with the manufacture's identification label attached to the nose of the car: Ford. Cousin Agnes placed her Mass card on the copper plate resting on a small table in front of the coffin. She walked over to the comfortable, wing-back chair, sat down, and stayed for the entire afternoon.

Aunt Esther carried in a large platter of turkey, piled high with equal amounts of dark and white meat, from the refrigerator in the back entry. She placed it on the dining room table. Ruby-red cranberry sauce arranged around the edges of the platter resembled leftovers served the day after Thanksgiving. The apple pies smelled of nutmeg and cinnamon with pastry so flaky that pieces of the crusts fell on to the pantry counter. The meringue adorning the top of a lemon pie glistened golden under the ceiling lamp. Missing one slice, I suspected the culprit to be my Uncle Bill, since that was his favorite dessert. The pecan pie, the best of all, tasted like candy. We asked my mother who made the pie. She couldn't remember, but this unknown cook, forever known as *The Pecan Pie Lady,* won our praises. To this day, Mary, Alicia, and I bake a pecan pie for the holidays.

The Rooney sisters, Eva and Ina, appeared at the front door crying, grasping each other's arms. Aunt Anna, Eva, and Ina were childhood friends. Mother tried to console these dear, sweet ladies. She ushered the grieving, pretty, gray-haired sisters into the parlor to join the other women dressed in black. They too brought a large plate of dark chocolate fudge.

I waited an interminable amount of time for the last mourner to leave the parlor and retreat to the dining room or kitchen for the ample repast. I glanced around for one last check. The room was now empty, except for me and Aunt Anna. I stepped up on the maroon velvet kneeler, stretched my body forward and touched my finger to her cheek. What did dead people feel like, I wondered? I wanted her face to be warm and soft, but it wasn't. It didn't move. I discovered that dead people have cool, hard skin. I jumped off the kneeler, looked around the room, and withdrew to the kitchen pantry to join up with Mary.

The choking smoke from cigars, stogies, pipes, and cigarettes floated into the pantry from the kitchen, barely noticed by Mary and me, as we delighted in sampling the wide variety of food that lay before us. We were not admonished for tasting anything. Unknowingly, Aunt Anna had given us free reign. The family's sorrow remained too deep for anyone to be concerned with our private feast.

A crestfallen Miss Emma Doolin entered the pantry and retrieved a plate of cookies to pass around. She was one of Aunt Anna's best friends, a fellow public health nurse, and classmate at Saint Joseph's Hospital.

The challenge that lay before Mary and me was the pickled tongue my Aunt Esther had ordered from Dave, the meat man, who arrived every other Monday at Aunt Esther's back door to sit and chat and take her meat order. Dave was Jewish and knew that every family gathering, be it a sad or happy occasion, called for pickled tongue. He told Aunt Esther it would make nice sandwiches and was a good keeper.

The tongue, a strange color of pink, not found in my Crayola box, lay unceremoniously atop the unadorned white, oval, porcelain meat platter. We examined it from all angles. The tongue appeared naked and ugly and strangely out of place among the more familiar food items. The dense, elongated piece of beef resembled a thirsty hound dog's tongue on a sultry summer day. Tiny outcroppings covered the entire surface of the skin looking like so many goose bumps.

"Mary, if I take a tiny bite, you have to promise to eat a little bit too."

Mary agreed, but only if I went first. I began by cutting a piece from the middle rather than the more offensive tip of the tongue. The long cutting knife resounded with a high-pitched squeak as I drew it through the tough flesh. Mary watched me chew and swallow the rubbery meat. Much to my surprise, I liked it.

"I'm not doing that. It's disgusting and you're weird for liking it," Mary huffed.

"Here try it."

I advanced with a piece of meat on the end of my fork and pushed it toward Mary's face.

Mary bolted and vanished into the kitchen crowd almost before I could finish my sentence.

Aunt Anna was the last family member to be waked in grandmother's front parlor.

I told my mother I missed my aunt not being at Dalton Street on our Sunday visits.

I recall my mother saying:

"Anita, life is change and if you do not adapt to it you will cease to live your life."

Without any discussion, I think my mother expected her nine-year-old daughter to understand what she had said. I guess I did. I still think about it today.

ORANGE IN THE TOE

Christmas Past

One Christmas I overheard my second oldest, Dan, tell his young son, Brendan, about the Christmas stocking he had as a child. Dan paused for a moment and then exclaimed,

"There was always an orange in the toe."

When I was growing up Santa could be counted on to put an orange in the toes of our Christmas stockings. I kept up this tradition with our four sons: Bill, Dan, Matt, and Tim.

Mine stretched from the fireplace mantel to the floor. Hidden in the lengthy stocking lay a bevy of surprises: a cookie press, a pin-on flashlight, a small purse, walnuts, ribbon candy, and so much more.

My sister, Alicia, looking for Santa

Before the excitement of Christmas morning there were things to be done. Each year my father drove to Sarki's, a small gas station in town, to purchase additional ornaments for the tree. All year long Sarki repaired cars, sold fuel, and a wide variety of automotive supplies. About the first week in December the dark, dingy front room of the station took on a festive air. The cans of oil and replacement windshield wipers were put to one side, making space for boxes of beautiful, gleaming, hand-painted tree ornaments. My father, no matter how many shiny balls we had for our tree at home, could not resist the temptation of purchasing more of these seasonal decorations. He bought a box or two each year.

Choosing the tree with my father and sisters signified a major annual event. The selection took time, close examination, and more money than was considered prudent, at least by my mother. The criteria was height, not fullness, with the tree always requiring a trimming to prevent it from scraping the ceiling.

"Let's not tell your mother what the tree cost," cautioned my dad before heading out on our adventure to a Christmas tree lot.

My mother never inquired, but she considered any price over ten dollars exorbitant. My father usually handed over a twenty-dollar bill to the vendor, receiving no change in return.

The week before Christmas we trudged up to the attic and carried down lights, the tree stand, and boxes and boxes of handsome ornaments collected over the years. Lights blinked on and off as my father tested each strand. My mother did not participate in decorating the tree. Sometimes she watched from afar or just vanished into the kitchen. My father strung the lights and hooked on ornaments that were out of our reach, but we did the rest.

When the tree was fully decked out my father called to my mother, "Ronnie, we're ready for the snow."

This invitation put my mother into action. We watched with

Mary and me Christmas morning with the tree covered in snow

anticipation as she poured two simple ingredients into a deep bowl: a box of Lux soap flakes and a gradual stream of warm water. The electric mixer whirled this simple concoction around and around in the bowl until it achieved the consistency of snow.

We immersed our hands into the fluff and spread the soft, white meringue along the outer edge of each branch. It took practice to avoid soap dollops from plummeting onto the carpet. My patient father, like an artist applying paint to a canvas, did the best job.

We inspected our work and then turned off all the living room and dining room lights, plugged in the extension cord, and admired what we thought to be the most beautiful Christmas tree in town, resplendent with freshly fallen snow. We repeated this evening activity of having the tree lights as the single illumination in the living room all during the holiday.

On Christmas Eve, Mary, Alicia, and I hung our flesh-colored, former school uniform stockings on the three permanent hooks attached to the fireplace. Reluctantly, my sisters and I went to bed for what we knew to be the longest night of the year.

The first activity in the wee hours of Christmas morning involved a trip to the bathroom. This special day did not excuse us from brushing our teeth. Having completed the task, we ran into the living room to unwrap the jungle of presents under the tree.

What we loved most involved digging deep into our cavernous stockings to discover the treasures that lay hidden behind the mysterious, bulging shapes. As always, in the toe of each stocking, lay a large, perfectly

Me and Mary, 1941

round orange. This anticipated "surprise" piece of fruit signified the end of a wondrous, fun-filled journey to the stocking's toe.

My mother sat in the green wing-back chair and my father on the flowered print sofa, watching us open our gifts. There were many wonderful real surprises: ice skates with plenty of room to grow into, a brand new Columbia bike, a Wedgwood blue wool bathrobe, and matching slippers. Mary received a rose-colored one, both sewed in secret by my mother. I loved the aqua doll cradle, decorated with decals, made by my dad in his downstairs workshop. The many memorable gifts we received over the years included a complete boxed set of much anticipated Uncle Wiggily books, a rubber doll I could bathe and feed, Monopoly, automatic Bingo, a Brownie Hawkeye camera, and much more. On occasion, a gift would not be to my liking. It most often was an article of clothing chosen by my mother. I pretended to be pleased so as not to disappoint my parents.

My father opened his gifts last. He piled the unopened presents on his lap, adjusting and rearranging them as his bounty increased.

"Come on, Dad, open just one. Let's see what you got," we pleaded.

He enjoyed holding on to his stack of gifts as if they were prize possessions. In time, he did open them. Slowly and deliberately he would untie the ribbon and pull back the scotch tape from the wrapping paper.

He cherished everything he received. I don't remember a year that his eyes did not brim with tears. The fluid just balanced there on the lower lids, only a blink away from streaming down his face, but this never happened. I knew that his emotional response to the gifts he received meant he loved being with his family, but also that something deeper was taking place.

Buying or making Christmas gifts for my father involved lots of thought and consideration. One year I sewed him a cotton, short-sleeved shirt. On Christmas morning he held it up for all to admire. I immediately noticed I had sewed one shirt panel with the print upside down. My father praised my skill and for years he wore the shirt with the jungle animals laying on their backs, legs jutting skyward, appearing to have been victims of a hunter's bullets.

My mother too received homemade gifts. One summer our neighbor across the street, Mrs. Overdeep, taught me how to embroider. Sitting in one of the comfortable wicker chairs on her front porch, I stitched a white linen cover to keep rolls warm. On one flap I embroidered in large, upper-case letters, HOT BUNS. My mother laughed when she read the message on the special gift I had made her, but she quickly composed herself and applauded my accomplishment.

I purchased a favorite Christmas gift for my father with money earned working part-time in college: a button-down, oxford-cloth, blue, long-sleeve dress shirt. After buying the shirt, a brown and blue diagonal striped tie in a display case caught my eye. I counted out my money for bus fare home, and there was just enough left in my billfold to buy the tie. It cost nine dollars. My father wore his new shirt and tie to church on Christmas morning. He looked very handsome sporting these new clothes with his best brown suit and just-polished brown shoes.

I knew that my father's childhood had been a lonely time. His mother, Marie Toutant LeClaire, died from tuberculous in her mid-twenties. My father and his younger brother, my Uncle Al, went to live with their grandmother and aunt for a brief time in Woonsocket, Rhode Island. When their aunt left to marry, the burden of bringing up two little boys proved too much for their grandmother. They were placed in an orphanage by their father, Thomas LeClaire.

My dad and Uncle Al lived in an all-boys home run by an order of French nuns. The location of the orphanage is thought be in Woonsocket.

Over the years, my mother quietly asked us not to make inquiries concerning this time in my dad's life since she felt it was just too sad. We obeyed and, therefore, know little about his early years. My dad did tell me that his father visited him only once during the several years he lived in the orphanage.

I do not know if they celebrated Christmas or had a big decorated tree for the boys to enjoy, but I like to think they did. I sometimes dream that the young children discovered a new pair of socks at the foot of their beds on Christmas morning and nestled inside was a big, perfectly round orange in the toe.

I wish I had said to my dad, "Will you tell me about Christmas when you and Uncle Al were little boys in the orphanage? Did Santa leave you any gifts? Did you have a tree or any thin, striped ribbon candy?"

Mary, Alicia, and I never asked any questions at all. The three of us regret that we did not inquire about his life in the orphanage. I think he would have liked to tell his daughters what happened during those early years. I hope my dad knows how we all would have loved to sit next to him and listen as he told us his story of so long ago.

Orange in the Toe is written in admiration, honor, and loving memory of my dad, (Joseph) Leo LeClaire.

BABY ALICE

Heartbreak

She wasn't a baby. I remember her when she was five years old and I was almost four. My family referred to my first and only cousin as Baby Alice so as not to confuse her with her namesake, my Aunt Alice. When we played, she was just Alice to me.

She belonged to that select group of 'only' children. This vulnerable lot of singles represented an enigma to me. Deep in my heart I felt their aloneness in the family structure to be pitied. Who was their solace when unjust punishment was administered, or you needed a companion to share a secret, borrow a pretty sweater, play Monopoly, or even engage in a scuffle? Alice and my other 'only' child friends fared very well, but I knew, though I never shared this with any of them, it was more fun to have sisters.

Alice, exactly to the day, three months older than my sister, Mary, was bright, read books, and put puzzles together at an early age. We were not jealous of her but reveled in the knowledge that we had a smart cousin.

She had dark green eyes that sparkled when she smiled, and a pretty, round face with blond hair rimmed with soft ringlets. One single bouncy curl fell softly on her forehead, much like Shirley Temple.

Baby Alice

My earliest memory of playing with my cousin remains vivid even today. The three of us roller skated around the bed in the room Mary and I shared. This otherwise prohibited indoor activity was ignored as my mother and Aunt Kay sat at the kitchen table and talked. They probably wanted time alone. We screamed and hollered and fell with skates clattering as we attempted to navigate around the room. The oak floor, covered with linoleum featuring nursery rhyme characters, was protected from any damage incurred by our skates with metal wheels.

The three cousins (l-r): Alice, Mary, and me

I remember running with Alice and Mary in her side yard in Rumford. Alice wore a navy blue coat with a bonnet trimmed in matching velvet. I noticed that 'only' children wore velvet more often than kids like us with more than one child in the family. They even donned these Sunday clothes for play like Alice did on this November day. We engaged ourselves in a nonsense game of running, our arms thrust out as if we were three birds gliding on an air current.

Around Christmas time of that year our cousin Alice contracted pneumonia. Dr. Kelly, her pediatrician and ours, made frequent visits to Aunt Kay and Uncle Bill's home to administer to Alice, but nothing seemed to help. On one such call Dr. Kelly prescribed some medicine that he felt would begin to turn things around.

Her health did not improve and he ordered blood tests. My aunt and uncle waited many anxious days for the results. They were stunned when they received the grim news. Alice had leukemia.

They made an appointment at Boston Children's Floating Hospital with a well known hematologist. They bundled Alice up for protection against a cold winter day and drove the thirty-mile trip to Boston.

The doctor examined my now frail, sick cousin. Tests were administered, more blood taken, and Alice was subjected to seemingly endless examinations. Again, they waited day after endless day for answers. On a return visit to Boston the doctor ushered my Aunt Kay and my Uncle Bill into his office. He informed them there was nothing further he could do for Alice's acute leukemia. He told them to go home, make her comfortable, and prepare for the worst. My bewildered aunt and uncle listened to the most unbearable news possible. They left the hospital and drove their precious child home to Rhode Island.

We visited her one Sunday afternoon hoping that Alice would be doing better and want to play with us. She sat in bed with lots of pillows propped up behind her head. A half-completed puzzle shifted on its board as she turned her head toward us and smiled. Mary and I hesitated in the doorway. She looked pale and her movements were slow. The adults spoke in hushed tones making me think that this manner of speaking was a harbinger of bad things to come. As young as I was that day, I knew our small family would never be the same again. Our playmate was drifting away from us and there was nothing we could do.

On Friday, May 23, 1941, Baby Alice died. She left behind a heartbroken mother and father, a grieving grandmother, aunts and uncles, and two sad young cousins.

I remember Alice lying motionless in her small casket in front of the shuttered, living room bay window. The white dress that Aunt Kay had purchased for her approaching First Communion lay smooth and still on her young body. We too, as if in solidarity, wore white dresses that my mother had made. The grownups stood around the room in silence except for the occasional soft-spoken words or a sob.

Mother sat with her arms around Mary and me on a bench a few feet from Alice's head. Mary whispered something to my mother and then slipped out of mother's embrace and walked up to Alice. She stood for a moment staring at our cousin. Mary reached into the casket and gave her shoulder a gentle nudge. She waited for an instant and then walked back to the bench.

"Alice is not sleeping. She won't wake up."

Mother gathered Mary and me in close to her side again. My mother leaned down and whispered to us,

"I have a secret to tell you both and I do not want you to tell anyone. Alice is in heaven and today she is an angel."

I don't recall questioning my mother's proclamation. I had never in my young life heard such beautiful words. I imagined Alice floating, smiling, dressed in a gown of the palest pink silk, the wings on her back wider and more majestic than any eagle gliding among the clouds. Her feathers, pure white, long, and perfect in every way, fluttered with a gentle beat that took Alice on a journey to any place she desired to go.

I never told anyone what my mother said to us that day until a few years ago when I divulged the secret to a long-time trusted friend who would understand. That sweet vision is still with me. I have only to close my eyes and I can see my cousin Alice.

She is so very near my Aunt Kay and my Uncle Bill, still adorned in pink, smiling, as she was in her life here on earth. A soft, blond, bouncy curl continues to fall lightly on to her forehead.

Post Script: Decades following Alice's death, my Aunt Kay read an article in *The New York Times* that reported the exact medicine she administered to Alice was causing World War II veterans to die of leukemia. They were given this same medicine many years after contracting malaria. The problem being, back in the time Alice was ill, the medical community did not know about child dosages. She was administered adult dosages of the medication causing the immediate onset of acute leukemia.

This story is dedicated, in loving memory, to my dear Aunt Kay and Uncle Bill and to our playmate, Alice.

*Picture taken shortly after my cousin
Baby Alice died
(l-r): My mother, Uncle Ed, Aunt Kay,
me, and Mary*

IN VOGUE

Thank You, Mom

My mother made this tan spring lightweight wool coat for me and I never got around to telling her how much I loved it.

It sported a very deep hem. The hand stitching along the hemline was very visible and the left set-in sleeve bunched somewhat, but these things did not bother me. The pockets were a great addition.

I always put on my brown felt bowler hat and brown shoes with socks that matched whenever I wore this favorite coat.

The sketch is copied from a picture my dad took of me in the backyard. I was nine.

LESSONS
Aunt Mary Esther Maguire

Esther as a baby

"All my friends are dying," exclaimed my Aunt Es.

I recall my insensitive response as if took place yesterday.

"Oh, Aunt Es, you always find new and younger friends," I replied.

Mary Esther Maguire was the very heart of our family. She saw nothing but good in her three nieces, Mary, Alicia, and me, and two nephews, Tom and Mike, and in just about everyone she encountered in her all-too-short, ninety-three years. She took an interest in everything we did. We were the children our maiden aunt never had.

On March 29, 1893, Mary Esther Maguire was brought into this world atop the Victorian walnut table in my grandparent's spacious kitchen. Every Maguire child, Aunt Esther told me, was delivered on that same oval table, except for my mother who was born in a hospital. This former birthing table now resides in my dining room.

I had the enviable position of being her godchild. I felt very special in this role. By some unwritten Aunt Esther rule, I received an extra Christmas gift and a second birthday cake from her, but she showered presents on all of us.

Her solid figure gave the outward appearance of being square, firm, and devoid of any waistline. I am sure, in some part, it was the result of her well-corseted figure, yet this almost immobile flesh-colored constraint oddly did not prevent her from feeling supple and inviting.

Easter Sunday, 1943
Mary, Aunt Esther, and me

Her plethora of freckles were an invitation for a young niece to feel her warm, tender-to-the-touch arm.

I spoke with both my sisters about this.

"I wrote a story about Aunt Es and I mentioned her skin."

"Oh," Mary replied in a hushed tone. "It was so soft, like a pillow filled with feathers. Remember? I loved her skin."

Alicia hesitated for a moment. "It was not so much her skin. I recall her being soft like the Pillsbury Dough Boy."

Her white, wavy, thick, cropped hair gave off a flash of blue in the right light. A daily application of indigo VO-5 hair conditioner, rubbed well into her scalp, produced this striking effect. Her eyes, as blue as an evening summer sky, appeared gentle and kindly.

On occasion she allowed her nieces to play beauty shop with her being the client. We applied lipstick well beyond her thin lip line and bedecked our good-natured aunt with a heavy application of eye shadow, rouge, and powder. She never wiped anything off in our presence. I can see her now preparing dinner in the pantry in her cotton housedress and full apron, looking very glamorous.

Esther loved clothes all her life

As a child I remember seeing a photograph of a young girl running a race outfitted in a polka-dot sweater and a long skirt to her ankles. Tight ringlets appeared to move and bounce even in the still black and white photograph. The back of the picture read, *Esther running for the City Club*.

Esther walked over a mile each day to and from Union Primary School in her hometown of Rumford, Rhode Island, and in 1911 she graduated from East Providence High School.

She attended secretarial school following graduation. My grandmother, a no-nonsense woman, told all her daughters:

"No man should have to support you. You will all have educations and be capable of making it on your own."

Esther went to work, I believe, in an office at one of the iron mills in Phillipsdale, a small manufacturing hamlet now on the National Registry of Historic Places. Phillipsdale was adjacent to Rumford, yet it was not considered a part of the larger town.

The Boy Friend

Sometime during her early working days, probably about 1918, Aunt Esther met a young doctor named Bill Bergan. They had a "spoken-for friendship," but no engagement ring. During their dating days my aunt heard Dr. Bergan had taken another woman out dancing. Aunt Es felt he had broken a trust. That did not sit well with her and she terminated the relationship.

Decades later, my aunt, standing in her living room reading the obituaries, said to no one in particular,

"Bill Bergan died today."

"Didn't you go with him?" I asked.

"Yes," she replied.

That was all she said. I inquired no further concerning her lost love.

I talked with my sister, Mary, about this ill-fated match and she replied,

"You know, Nita, I don't think Bill Bergan ever married and the one time I talked with Aunt Es about him I sensed a tone of regret in her voice."

A New Life

Several years following the death of my grandfather, John Simon Marguire, on November 19, 1928, Aunt Esther found her life taking an unexpected turn that was not of her choosing. She left her job in Phillipsdale because my grandmother needed assistance due to illness. Aunt Anna and Uncle Ed, both unmarried, worked and continued to live in the family home at 49 Dalton Street in Rumford.

The job of keeping the house, tending the many flower beds, the vegetable garden, and especially the increasing demands of caring for my grandmother fell to Aunt Esther. Hers was now a life of cooking, cleaning, ironing, and entertaining family and friends. She saw to it that my grandmother, following a stroke, was washed, fed, dressed, and spotless in every way. My aunt referred to anyone who experienced a stroke as having a shock. This local idiom for stroke escaped me as being inaccurate medical terminology. As a child, I believed the two words to be interchangeable.

Aunt Es considered the beginning of the week laundry days, though she did not own a washing machine until many years later. She did much of the wash using a rippled aluminum and wooden scrubbing board. The What Cheer Laundry Company picked up the remaining soiled clothes and sheets every other week. She stuffed these items in a large, mesh bag secured with an over-sized chrome safety pin and placed it on the rear steps. In a few days the clean laundry arrived back, wrapped in brown butcher paper and tied with string, looking like so many unopened gifts.

The ironing board stayed in the closet until Tuesday, ironing day. Aunt Es snapped the wooden legs into position and placed it in the center of the kitchen. She plugged the iron's long, black cord into an open socket hanging down from the kitchen light.

I remember ironing day as being a social event of sorts. If friends dropped by, they usually sat on one of the straight-backed, wooden spindle kitchen chairs and chatted, laughed, and enjoyed a cup of tea. As children the electric iron did not interest us, but we did find the heavy, black flat iron a curiosity. Aunt Es placed it on top of the hot end of the imposing wood-burning cast-iron stove. It required that you grasp the handle with a pot holder as a protection for your hand and iron quickly before it cooled down. She sprinkled the clothes using a glass bottle filled with water that held a little metal sprinkle-head on top. Like a skater, the weighty, black iron glided over my Uncle Ed's damp, starched dress shirts under the expertise of my aunt's skillful hand.

The backyard clothesline, (not the usual cotton rope variety, but a substantial wire one), was secured to the grape arbor on one end and attached to a cedar post supporting a bird house on the other. Two tall, sturdy clothes poles held the line high out of harm's way. New Englanders, a thrifty bunch, liked things, such as a metal clothesline, to last forever.

Tending to my ailing grandmother constituted a full-time job, but now Aunt Esther faced a new, heartbreaking responsibility. Her younger sister Anna's health began to deteriorate. Only in her fifties, it soon became apparent that she could no longer continue to work as a public health nurse. Aunt Es and Aunt Anna were close in age and the best of friends. Now Aunt Es, the younger of the two, found herself caring for her big sister.

We never got the full health story on anyone. The family kept secrets. My sister Mary and I tried our best, snooping around corners, or pretending not to listen to adult conversations, but information did not come our way very often. Mother did tell us that Aunt Anna had acute kidney problems.

Poor Aunt Es, doing double duty, could not depend on my mother and my Aunt Kay on a regular basis, since they both had families, and my mother, like her sister Es, did not drive. Kay taught school full time. My Aunt Alice worked in New York City and did come home on occasion. Aunt Esther had many friends that she depended on, but mostly for friendship. Sometimes Mary and I visited my aunt to help, but we were mostly company and fun for her. She enjoyed having us around. I never heard her say that she was bone weary or could use some help.

Her greeting to us upon our arrival remained the same.

Aunt Esther holding Alicia. She loved visits from her nieces and nephews.

"Ronnie, come on in. Where's Leo? Mary, my darling, you're getting so tall. Anita, my darling, how are you?"

She did not wait for a response but encircled us in a loving embrace. When Alicia came along, Aunt Es would bend down and hug our little sister with such enthusiasm that Alicia appeared to vanish in the folds of her apron and housedress.

Not long into our visit my mother often shooed us out the back door.

"You girls go out and play. Esther and I want to talk."

This seemed to be my mother's singular solution once we began to be an annoyance.

Adventures with Tommy & Mike

There were no toys to play with at my grandmother's house inside or outside. Not a doll, not a scooter, or even a ball. A dusty croquet set, leaning against a wall in the garage, remained unused. We never took it out even to whack a ball with a mallet. Croquet seemed like a game that grownups would play following a picnic in the side yard. It didn't garner our interest.

The lack of toys did not deter us. There were apple trees to climb and grapes on the arbor. We sucked out the sweet juice from under the skin and spit the slimy, gelatinous interior as far as we could. When in bloom, we picked lilacs that grew in abundance along one side of the yard. We examined the huge rhubarb plants at the end of the vegetable garden, wondering how far we could chew along the tart-tasting stalk before mistakenly biting into the poisonous leaf, causing one of us to die on the spot. Sometimes we would walk over to visit a neighbor on the next street who always invited us in and treated us to cookies and milk at her kitchen table. We loved to play with our friend, Peter, who lived down the hill across the street from Omega Pond. We knocked on doors of neighbors, uninvited, and invariably they would ask us in. Aunt Esther knew everyone.

The real adventure began at the two small buildings beyond the grape arbor in the backyard: one, an old two-seater outhouse and the other a larger shed used to conceal the garbage and trash cans. Both these buildings were painted white with green trimming to match the shutters of the house. The garbage house, our main source of fun, kept us busy until we were called in for dinner. We played this game only when my cousins Tom and Mike were visiting.

We took turns to see who could stay in the shed the longest. The first "volunteer" usually was pushed into the shed. The putrid smell of the rotting garage, especially in the summertime, made our game, we thought, one of courage and tenacity. The ones left outside, pressing their bodies against the door, counted one, two, three, while the prisoner, usually screaming, endured the smell as long as possible. The cousin who persevered the longest was determined the winner. No one ever told us to stop, nor did it occur to us that it might be a strange way to spend a Sunday afternoon.

Sometimes, when we tired of the garbage shed, we went down to the white picket fence at the very end of the yard. We leaned against it, talking very loudly. Aunt Esther told us that Houdini's assistant lived in the house directly behind my grandmother's. We fully expected this unknown man to throw open a window and execute an amazing magic trick. This never happened, but we felt sure if we stayed at the fence staring at his house and making enough noise, we might attract his attention.

Aunt Es Cares for my Aunt Anna and my Grandma Kate

Aunt Anna was in and out of the hospital, and my grandmother was now bedridden. Aunt Es had little time to herself. Uncle Ed worked all day and I am sure helped her, but only if he was asked to assist in some way. Mostly, she did everything that had to be done. She knew her family could be called on and my aunt enjoyed frequent visits by her many friends, but day in and day out, her indomitable spirit, energy, faith, and positive attitude kept her going.

My grandmother died following years of excellent care, good food, and attention to all her needs. She lived to the age of eighty nine.

Grandma was waked in the front parlor opposite the three windows that looked out on Dalton Street. The casket, lined in soft, cream-colored taffeta, cushioned her slim body. She looked comfortable, just relaxing there, without her familiar black eye patch. A gold circular pin held the neck of her batiste flowered dress concealing the small hole in her neck, the result of a goiter (an abnormal enlargement of the thyroid gland) operation many years prior. Just beyond the front porch, the tiny 'Thousand Petal' pink roses she planted so many years ago were in full bloom. An ornate purple crepe hung on the solid wood door.

A young John McManus

Mourners came in a steady stream to pay their respects to Kate Maguire. That evening Aunt Es, weary from a full day, walked to the front hall to switch off the porch light. There was a knock on the door. She peered though the leaded glass and saw the tall, slim figure of John McManus. He was dressed in a black suit and tie and she could make out that he held his black bowler respectfully over his heart. She opened the door.

"Good evening, Esther. I have come to pay my respects to Mrs. Maguire and offer my services to stay watch overnight with the body."

Aunt Es knew John McManus, a cousin, but not well. A twenty-four hour watch over the body was a common practice among the Irish when someone died. The body never remained unaccompanied, day or night. Aunt Es had planned on my Uncle Ed and my Aunt

Alice to take shifts through the night and she would arise early to sit with Momma until her sisters, Veronica and Katherine, arrived after breakfast.

She invited John McManus inside and he knelt on the kneeler alongside the casket and bowed his head in silent prayer for the soul of Catherine Lynch Maguire. He stood up. Aunt Esther, in an uncharacteristic move, without consulting anyone, said, "John, I would be happy to have you stay through the night. Help yourself to the pies in the pantry and there is milk in the refrigerator."

Aunt Es, Aunt Alice, and my Uncle Ed had a good night's sleep while John McManus sat in the parlor for the two-night vigil looking after Grandma.

I remember my mother saying to me not long after Grandma died, "I think what meant the most to Es, caring for Momma all those years, was that Momma never suffered from a bed sore or any skin irritation anywhere on her body. Her skin was smooth as silk."

This was a bit difficult for a young child to grasp and to understand its significance, but I do remember my mother and my aunts rolling white cloths in the shape of a donut and placing them, with care, under the heels of my grandmother's long, bony feet.

Two years following Grandma's death, on January 19, 1947, Aunt Anna died. Aunt Es afforded her the same loving and tender care.

Dawning of a New Day

Now at age fifty four Aunt Es knew her time had arrived.

One Monday morning she put on her best navy blue print dress, navy coat, and matching hat with a small, delicate veil decorating the front rim. She laced her sturdy, church shoes and slipped on a pair of white cotton gloves. Aunt Es headed down Dalton Street hill and waited for the yellow United Electric Rail, known to everyone as the UER bus, for the five-mile trip into downtown Providence.

Aunt Es told me many years later that she only applied for two jobs. The first was at the Shepard Company Department store and the second at The Outlet Company for a position in the business office. The Outlet Company wasn't an outlet as we know the term today, but a very complete department store selling everything from fine furniture to cosmetics. It was the largest department store in the state, formed in 1891 and opened as a department store at 176 Weybosset Street in downtown Providence. It closed in 1982 and was destroyed by fire in 1986.

The Outlet Co.: Left, as I remember it: right, as it burned in October, 1986

Aunt Es said she sat for a brief time in the fifth-floor waiting room outside the manager, Mr. Saul Logowitz's, office. He called my Aunt Es in for her interview and they exchanged pleasantries. She told him about her working background so many, many years ago.

"Are you a Catholic?"

"Why, yes, I am," replied Aunt Es, not the least bit puzzled by his inquiry.

"Good," said Mr. Logowitz, "I like Catholic girls in my office. I find they are hard and loyal workers. I would like you to start on Thursday, Esther, and you will be trained as a comptometer operator." (A comptometer was the first commercially successful key-driven mechanical calculator.)

So began a very happy time in my aunt's life. Her fellow workers became her extended family. Mary, Alicia, and I visited her often at her fifth-floor office. We knew the names and faces of so many of her fellow workers and they treated us as kindly as if we were their nieces too.

Aunt Es enjoyed treating us to lunch, usually at Edith's Lunch Room. Edith's was a small, one-room restaurant two streets over from The Outlet. Once there you had the option of climbing three flights of narrow, steep stairs or taking the old, swaying, partially open elevator. I usually opted for the stairs, huffing and puffing as I reached the top landing. The room, hot and crowded and particularly unpleasant on a rainy day, reeked of peeled, hard-boiled eggs. Even though the smell made me queasy, I always opted for the egg salad sandwich with a pickle on the side and a glass of milk.

Edith, we were told, had family obligations and was continually in financial distress. Aunt Es felt she had an obligation to support Edith in her troubles by having lunch at her establishment. I never said it, but I did wonder if our sandwiches would really keep Edith from going out of business.

Nantucket

How my aunt loved that island. She knew it from one end to the other. For a few years she asked Mary and me to join her on vacation. Mary went one year for a week and I was her companion the next.

Dad drove us in the early morning hours to New Bedford. We boarded the ferry *Nobska* for the long, and often rough sail to the island. Woods Hole was the first stop to bring on more passengers and cars before heading out to sea. My mother packed a hearty lunch for us to enjoy en route. We ate early to insure that we would be hungry by the time we docked. The first stop, once on land, always included a meal at *The Skipper.*

The Skipper, an old dry-docked sailboat several feet from the boat landing, made what we thought was the best chicken pot pie in the world. Our selection never changed. It arrived in ceramic bowls, always too hot to eat. Steam rose from the perfect circular vent in the center of high, flaky crust. Impatient and hungry, I always managed to burn my tongue on the first bite.

Following our tasty meal, we lugged our wheel-less suitcases down the road where Aunt Es hailed a taxi for the short trip to The Cliff Lodge, our home for the week.

Nantucket: The Cliff Lodge

The Cliff Lodge, built in 1771 as a whaling master's home, faced toward the Nantucket Sound. Situated on the crest of Cliff Road, the three-story quintessential island home, with its grey, weathered cedar shingles, and breathtaking views, catered mostly to older couples and single ladies.

Some years we stayed in a ground-floor room. A fireplace on one wall was so enormous I could stand up or sit on the chair in the cavernous opening. This became a favorite spot to read or sketch. To keep me busy Aunt Es bought me a pad and pencils on one of our many shopping trips along Main Street.

Another year we had a room on the second floor facing the Nantucket Sound. It was fun peering out the window watching sailboats dart across the azure blue water. This all-white room featured white walls, bedspread, and windows adorned in fine organdy curtains that bellowed and swayed in the breeze. Aunt Es reminded me often about keeping the room clean and in perfect condition. I preferred the ground floor lodging where things were casual and without any rules at all.

*Me and Aunt Es, getting ready to dye her bathing suit, cousin
Florence, Alicia, and my mother at Dalton St., Rumford*

Going to the beach took the entire day. This involved catching the un-air-conditioned beach bus for the one-hour long, hot, stop-and-go ride to the ocean. I remember sitting across from Aunt Es examining her outfit in detail. She wore an oversized beach cover-up, carried a large pocketbook, and a brightly colored, striped canvas bag that hung uneasily over one shoulder. Her old-style droopy, rayon knit, navy, ill-fitting bathing suit remained hidden under her cover-up.

Arriving at the beach, we ambled around searching for the perfect spot to spread out our towels. She tucked her grey hair under a snug-fitting bathing cap and then I assisted her getting out of the terry robe. We walked across the pleasingly warm sand, with me trailing a short distance behind. Aunt Es waded up to her ankles in the chilly Atlantic, content to be splashing about in the shallow water. She never went out far enough to get her suit or even her kneecaps wet.

Every year prior to the Nantucket trip, Aunt Es purchased navy dye to soak her only bathing suit in an oval, chipped, enamel tub in the Dalton Street side yard. The unremarkable result of this annual ritual achieved a slightly deeper shade of blue.

Sometimes during our Nantucket week, we took the bus to Siaconset, a seaside community on the far eastern rim of the island. The small, picturesque, charming, rose-covered clapboard cottages were reminiscent of paintings taken from a child's picture book. At the water's edge I climbed and jumped from one boulder to the next while Aunt Es kept a keen eye on my escapades.

The Nobska *Ferry*

"Anita, dear, be careful. Take care not to slip and topple into the water. I don't know what I'd say to your mother if you did."

My aunt worried about me because, not having children of her own, she was unaware that this was how thirteen-year-olds behaved.

One year a nor'easter blew in for an entire week when we were living down in the dark ground-level accommodations. To keep our spirits up we took a taxi each day all over the island to different spots. Once out of the cab, the rain and wind pelted and battered us about.

The storm was beginning to abate as we boarded the *Nobska* for the trip home, but not enough for a smooth sail. The seas were rough; whitecaps smashed against the side of the boat as it rolled to the right and then to the left. I liked sitting outside under the wooden awning watching the wild sea.

After hours of enduring our bumpy sail, I could see Woods Hole in the distance. The ferry tacked to and fro several times as it attempted to dock. Approaching the landing was an extraordinarily difficult task in the inclement weather, since Woods Hole is known as being one of the most dangerous ports on the east coast. We began to weave and bob toward the shore, but not in the direction of the dock. We lurched and drifted sideways, eventually coming to a long grinding halt alongside the rocky and heavily treed shoreline.

I jumped up to get a better view as trees slapped against the side of the boat and began to protrude at odd angles onto the walkways. Aunt Es called me back to stay in my chair out of harm's way.

Soon the captain came on the public-address system and announced he had missed the landing and we had gone aground. The restaurant, he said, would remain open and that we all must wait patiently for the tide to come in to float us out again for a retry at docking.

After many long and boring hours, the engines produced a deafening roar and we were underway. The captain made a second attempt to come into Woods Hole. It was successful and soon we were off to our final destination, New Bedford.

As we got close to the landing dock, I leaned over the railing and was able to see my father waiting by the harbor building. He was a welcome sight. I think my dad must have been weary, too. He had been on time for our scheduled arrival, only to learn that the *Nobska* had gone aground. Impatient, he drove all the way back to Riverside and returned for our new docking time, a 128-mile round-trip drive for him that day.

Christmas on Dalton Street

Christmas was a major occasion. About mid-afternoon on Christmas day, we left Riverside and journeyed the few miles to Rumford for our family celebration. Mike, Tommy, Uncle Bill, and Aunt Kay joined us at Dalton Street for the festivities. Gifts were laid out on the floor and spilled into the middle of the living room rug. It was an amazing sight, especially for a child. We were sure we received more Christmas gifts than anyone in the entire world.

Aunt Es did not have a tree until we were teenagers but, just prior to Christmas, Uncle Ed went to the attic and carried down a full-sized cardboard fireplace with real wood trim for its mantel. Aunt Es filled and hung a second Christmas stocking for each of her nieces and nephews. Each stocking had the requisite orange in the toe. We opened gifts, one after another, while Uncle Ed busied himself gathering the wrinkled and torn gift paper and ribbon to be used the following year. Knowing my aunt and how she loved Christmas, I doubt if the wrappings ever appeared again. Most of the gift box tops sported a large *O* in the center, the logo of The Outlet Company.

A light dinner followed in the dining room. The menu remained the same year after year: sliced turkey sandwiches with cranberry sauce, various condiments, and apple and mincemeat pie for dessert. A slice of sharp cheddar cheese, much to the disappointment of the children, garnished each slice. We would have preferred a scoop of ice cream.

Tommy standing, Mary, Mike, and me in 1942, Christmas at Dalton Street

Retirement: One More Adventure

In 1961 Aunt Es had a mild heart attack and her doctor recommended she retire. The family home was sold and my aunt moved into a small apartment. My dad read about a new ten-story building slated to be built near Rumford for people with low incomes. He encouraged Aunt Esther to apply and she did. She was one of the first occupants of City View, a Housing and Urban Development project. Aunt Es chose a sunny, one-bedroom apartment on the top floor that faced east toward the then quiet, picturesque countryside of Seekonk, Massachusetts. My aunt made friends wherever she went and this was no exception. She enjoyed every day of her eighteen years at City View.

Aunt Es loved our four boys (Bill, Dan, Matt, and Tim) and their Boston cousins the McCarthys (Andrea, Kris, Peter, and Danny). She always baked Special K chocolate chip cookies and packed them to the brim in a round, metal tin for our family's long trip back to Baltimore.

When Aunt Es was in her eighties, she accompanied our family home from our vacation in Rhode Island to Maryland. She enjoyed partaking in our ordinary daily activities. One Sunday afternoon my husband crowded us into the station wagon for a short trip to the fields behind the boys' elementary school. The clear fall day, crisp and windy, made for a perfect afternoon to fly the new Mylar kite my husband, Bill, had brought home from a business trip to San Francisco. The dog barked and jumped and darted about. The boys yelled and ran grasping the ball of string, attempting to control the kite as it flashed in the brilliant sunshine. It soared skyward and just as quickly dipped into a nose dive, plunging to the ground. Aunt Es laughed and called out to the boys and appeared to be enjoying it as much as any child flying that elusive, powerful kite. We all had such a good time that day and my aunt spoke of that fun-filled afternoon for years.

At the end of the week, I accompanied Aunt Es back home. It was her very first airplane ride. As we approached New York City, the pilot came on the public address system.

"This is an exceptional night. You don't very often see New York City like this. I am coming in to give you the best view."

The pilot banked the plane and Aunt Es saw the city from the air with thousands of dazzling lights and a radiant red and blue sunset that appeared to outline every skyscraper. We watched in wonder until we could see no more.

Aunt Es was getting on in years and one night she rolled out of bed and fell, hitting her head on the sharp corner of her old hope chest. Not long after she stumbled again and landed in her closet. She laid on the closet floor all through the night. Her love of shopping and extensive wardrobe saved her from injury and made for a soft landing, but she could not get up. In the morning Aunt Es was able to reach the telephone and call my Aunt Kay. An ambulance was summoned, but she refused to get in.

My sister, Mary, and brother-in-law, Jim, came down from Boston. Mary looked at her dear aunt and said, "Aunt Es, I am packing your bags and you are coming back to Milton with us."

Aunt Esther was thrilled: another adventure.

She spent two months on a temporary bed in the McCarthy den. It was a difficult situation for Mary and Alicia, since the lovely, old home did not have a tub or shower on the first floor. Mary took care of Aunt Es all day and Alicia arrived in the early evening coming from work, north of Boston, to get Aunt Es ready for bed.

Mary and Alicia tended to our aunt's increasing needs, no different from the many years they cared for our mother, Aunt Alice, and Aunt Kay with devotion, kindness, and skill. I know it was very difficult at times due to Alicia's job and Mary caring for her young family. They loved these women, as did I, and enjoyed their friendship and company. These special Maguire women never failed to show their gratitude. They were a blessing in our lives.

Aunt Es experienced a few heart attacks while at the McCarthy's and spent brief stays at Milton Hospital. Alicia and Mary determined that Aunt Es, weakened from her heart attacks, needed twenty-four-hour care. They searched for the best nursing home they could find.

Now ninety-three years old, Aunt Esther made another adjustment to her living arrangements. She entered a nursing home and became fast friends with her roommate in the month she lived there. One day when everyone was out of the room Aunt Esther, sitting in a chair alongside her bed, bowed her head and fell into her final sleep.

Not long ago, I came across the last letter written by Aunt Es to me a few days before she died. The brief note was written with steady, legible handwriting. Her message was true to herself to the very end.

Dear Anita,

I am enclosing a small check for the boys. I know your time is precious, but I could not forget them. I am glad you had a nice holiday. (I) will send you my phone number after Monday.

Love to you all. Aunt Esther

This is the last Christmas card to my family from my Aunt Es

IN VOGUE

Just Like Heidi

I felt like a girl from a foreign land when I donned this favorite dress. It reminded me of something Heidi would have worn climbing the high meadow to her grandfather's mountain home.

The deep green and yellow plaid skirt and white blouse took on an international flair with the front laced-up vest. I dressed for school without effort in this all-in-one-piece dress.

This much-loved cotton dress was just one of many gifts that our beloved Aunt Esther gave to Mary, Alicia, and me over the years.

I asked my mother to save this treasured outfit for me after I outgrew it. I guess she forgot. It was nowhere to be found when I poked around the attic several years later.

GOD'S LITTLE HELPERS
The Art of the Deal

For years my mother washed, starched, and ironed the enormous white linen altar cloths, as well as dozens of small, cotton, accordion-folded finger towels for our church. These little towels were used by the priest during Mass to dry his fingers after the pouring of water.

Alicia liked to iron the narrow, accordion-pleated napkins, and so did I, but after completing three or four we became discouraged and begged our mother to complete the task. At first glance, it appeared easy and intriguing, but we found that skill and patience were necessary.

My mother carried out this formidable laundry chore with personal strings attached. She had made a bargain with God. She promised to pray daily and to do the church washing and ironing, but for a price: my mother asked God to grant a special intention in return. The combination of manual labor in conjunction with her daily prayers seemed reasonable and fair to my practical mother.

She was a woman of faith, purpose, stamina, and true to her word, my mother always completed the church linens on time. The delivery of the linens, not part of her Godly deal, fell to Mary, Alicia, and me. Alicia, being the youngest, did not take the sizable altar cloths, but walked to church carrying a well-worn shoe box filled with exactly one dozen sparkling, white, folded finger towels.

Carting the ample, clean, starched altar linens demanded muscular control, patience, and a fair amount of luck.

"Here, Anita, return these two altar cloths to church. Be careful. Look out! You're stepping on the hem."

The familiar routine required that my arms be held straight and outstretched in front of me. With utmost care, my mother draped the altar linens over my two limbs.

"Anita, separate your arms a little more. Good, that is just about right."

Her precise instructions regarding the portage of these cloths could put the fear of God in anyone. She opened the back door and the arduous journey began.

For some unknown reason it did not bother me trekking by my friends' homes: Patty, Lianne, Nancy, and (most importantly) the neighborhood heart-throb, Fuffa. I forged forward carrying out my assignment, looking not unlike the female equivalent of a stiff-armed Frankenstein.

My endurance, tested to its limits, entailed one more hurdle. To gain entrance into the church, the door handle had to be turned without causing my load to shift and slide off my now aching arms. Bending at the knees, with my right hand in alignment with the entry knob, I gave it a slow, decisive turn while at the same time delivering a quick kick to the bottom of the door. This method never failed to work.

Once inside, I put my cargo atop the linen press. The altar cloths were then placed flat in the long, shallow drawer, all ready to be used when needed.

Mary and I were altar cleaners as well as linen transporters. We both assisted the nuns in dusting and polishing the worship space. I had the additional responsibility of preparing the vestments each Tuesday for evening novena. This allowed me to skip last period music, avoiding the unbearable exercise of reading notes aloud with my class.

It was a double-edged sword getting out of music. Escaping class was fun, but entering the cold, dimly lit, empty church remained creepy, even in midday, for an eleven-year old. The trip from school to church took only minutes. I walked out the school front gate, crossed

Smith Street, darted behind the rectory, and entered the side door of the church. Checking my surroundings was imperative. Pausing to glance down at the dark and foreboding narrow stairway leading to the church basement caused me to pick up my pace.

I raced up the stairs, flipped on the light switch, and walked out onto the altar. The afternoon sun cast streams of brilliant light through the multicolored stained-glass windows. The dazzling array of jewel tones momentarily captured my attention. The church was empty.

The side closet in the vestibule held the alb. I took it off the hanger and placed the garment on top of the linen press, face down. The cincture that wrapped around the priest's waist came next, with instructions from one of the nuns to form the letter *M* with the cording, which I guess stood for Mary. The heavy, silk, lined chasuble from the second drawer comprised the final item on the small stack of vestments: everything now in proper sequence for the priest to slip into his novena clerical robes.

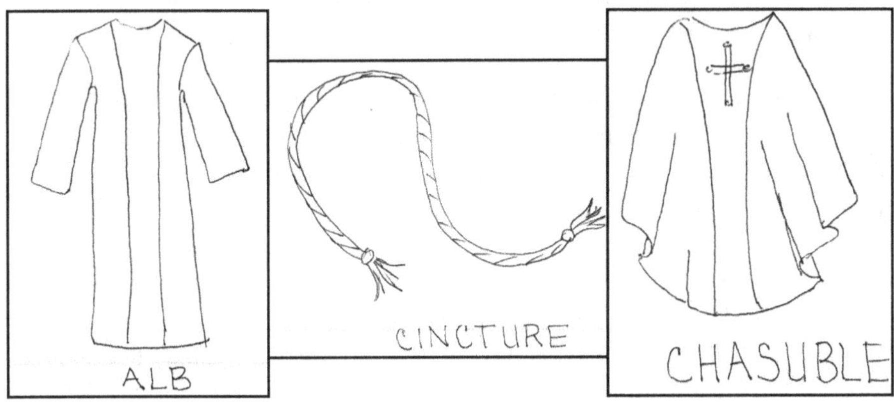

The stole that the priest wore over his shoulders and hands while raising the elaborate, gold, monstrance containing the white host, was wide, long, and silky. This presented a challenge. It required that three pleats were fashioned on each side before its placement over the back of the shiny, varnished side altar bench. I grasped it, put it in its proper place, and almost as if on cue, it slid off the bench with lighting speed and slumped in a pile on the floor. I repeated my task.

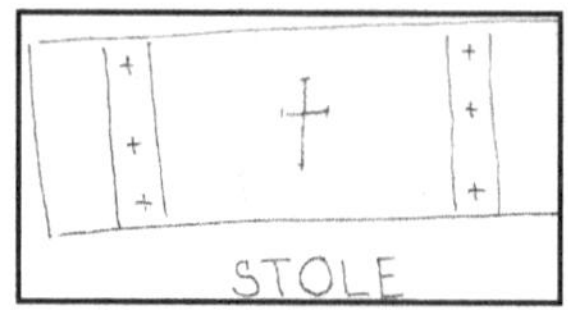

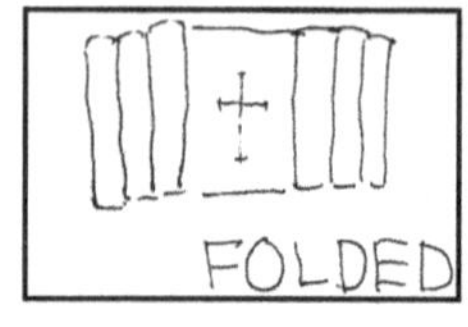

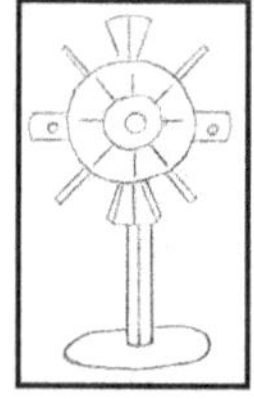

Monstrance

Having completed my church duties, I turned off the light and started out the side door, hesitating for a moment, and then hurried back to the altar. The stole had taken its familiar and predictable route. It needed refolding again. I performed my duty once more. This time, I charged down the stairs, exited the church, and stepped out into the sunshine.

Sometime around 1950 there was an industrial revolution of sorts: polyester! The linens were replaced with the easy-to-care-for material and my mother's major washing and ironing mission abruptly came to an end. The new "linens" never looked as formal, white, and crisp as when my mother prepared them. She continued to iron the pleated finger towels and Alicia delivered them to church until she graduated from St. Brendan's School.

My mother now believed that her bargaining had come to fruition and she ended her churchly task. She told us from the outset that her wish was that my father, when it was his time to die, would be blessed with the grace of a happy death.

The term "happy death" was used often in the Catholic Church. It seems like a contradiction in terms to me, but it refers to having your loved one not experience a lengthy suffering prior to death and to receive the Last Rights of the Church.

Mother said that Dad had experienced a sad and lonesome childhood growing up in an orphanage. She did not wish him to endure a prolonged struggle at the end of his life.

My dad died October 17, 1965. He was ill for just ten days.

VERONICA AND VERA

Courage: the right thing

My mother walked the half mile to St. Brendan's church to attend daily Mass on most days, but a good nor'easter or a major snowstorm did keep her home. On those days she silently recited her morning prayers in the comfortable forest green upholstered chair in the living room, situated next to the front windows.

Mother's brisk pace, aided by her no-nonsense black, lace-up pumps kept her sure-footed traversing Turner Avenue's uneven sidewalks. A small, unobtrusive felt hat, secured by a long, lethal hat pin, kept it securely in place. This covering of a woman's head put her in compliance with one of the many Catholic Church rules.

July 10, 1957, had the promise of a pleasant summer day. The morning haze coming in off Narragansett Bay hung low, but soon vanished when the sun peeked out behind the clouds.

St. Brendan's Church

93

My mother and several other worshipers discovered the main entrance to the church locked. Their unrelenting loud knocking eventually brought the janitor around to the front. He explained that in the early hours of the morning a stubborn, smoky fire had started in the basement, apparently due to faulty wiring. The interior of the church sustained heavy damage, yet the outside of the building gave no hint that anything out of the ordinary had taken place.

It was quickly learned that Captain McPherson, of the Riverside Fire Department, had died of smoke inhalation while attempting to escape from the basement. Captain McPherson had no familiarity with the building, since he did not belong to St. Brendan's parish. He unknowingly walked into a smoke-filled cloakroom located directly across from the basement auditorium door. Captain McPherson entered the unlit, narrow room where he collapsed and died at the end of the long passage with no outlet. The door to the stairway leading to the outside was to the left.

On the following Sunday, the congregation gathered to attend Mass in the school auditorium. Father Tierney, the pastor, talked at length about the fire and, in his ramblings, he inferred that Captain McPherson should have known the doorway he used was not an exit.

My mother leaned forward, fighting back tears, as his cruel words spilled over her. Stone-faced, she riveted her eyes on him in disbelief as he spoke from his makeshift pulpit. How could any human being, she thought, be so insensitive, so ill informed, and above all, so unchristian?

My mother, incensed and embarrassed, took it upon herself to visit Mrs. McPherson and extend condolences from the members of St. Brendan's parish. She feared that the grieving family would somehow hear about the remarks made from the altar on the previous Sunday. She called and asked Mrs. McPherson if she could pay her a call. Mother did not know the family, but knew the house well, since she walked by the small, white, frame dwelling each morning on her way to church.

Mrs. McPherson, a slim, petite, pretty woman, a few years my mother's junior, extended a warm welcome. The two women talked for some time in the compact front parlor crowded with a variety of over-stuffed furniture. The southwest window provided a partial view of the square, grey church tower in the distance. In conversation, Mrs. McPherson affectionately referred to her husband as "The Captain." He was 51 years old and left behind his wife, two teenage children, and her ailing father. The widow's pension would barely provide for the family's needs. The care of her frail, elderly father prevented her from seeking outside employment.

As my mother was leaving, she noticed some deep-green, wool gabardine fabric on the dining room table with tissue paper pattern pieces pinned to the material. My mother said that she, too, was a sewer. Mrs. McPherson held up her project. It was a winter storm coat for her daughter. The sleeves were waiting to be cut out, but the main body of the coat was complete. Perfectly made bound buttonholes adorned the front panel. The collar and front facings were interfaced, giving the coat proper stiffness and body. My mother was amazed. The coat had the fine detail and construction of a garment found in the shop of a skilled tailor. Mother inquired if Mrs. McPherson would be willing to give sewing lessons if she found some young girls interested in receiving instruction. Mrs. McPherson agreed. Veronica, my mother, turned and gave a warm embrace to her new friend, Vera.

I was in her first sewing class along with three of my friends: Bette, Barbara, and Carlotta. Under Mrs. McPherson's direction, we learned to do our very best on every project, and to construct garments that had a high level of difficulty to enable us to learn new skills. We made coats, jackets, kilts, dresses, and slacks. We matched plaids. We picked out stitches that were incorrect. We made bound buttonholes and learned proper pattern placement and, above all, not to waste fabric. Lessons were taken seriously, but our talking and laughter could always be heard above the hum of the sewing machines. Our instruction continued for a few years. Mrs. McPherson had many pupils, including my youngest sister, Alicia, and her friends after we had gone on to college, careers, and marriage.

My mother tried to right a wrong. She took her words and put them into action. Mrs. McPherson carried on without "The Captain" in her life. Her good nature made you feel better for having been in her company.

There were two heroines in this story, but Captain Robert McPherson, the real hero, paid the ultimate price, his life in the line of duty.

This story is dedicated to my talented, cheerful, friend, Mrs. McPherson, and her husband, "The Captain."

JONATHAN JO

Downstairs Dad

Mother read to us at bedtime. She often recited a favorite of hers, "Jonathan Jo," a poem by A.A. Milne.

It told the story of an old man and a young boy. Jonathan Jo's talents were limitless. He could produce anything the young boy requested. This reminded me of my dad.

Jonathan Jo
Has a mouth like an 'O'
And a wheelbarrow full of surprises;
If you ask for a bat,
Or something like that
He has got it whatever the size is.

My dad did not resemble the old man illustrated in the poem, but he was clever and smart and could build anything you asked him to, not unlike Jonathan Jo.

Dad made a living for our family of five as an erecting engineer. He designed and supervised the construction of large machines that dried a variety of products, mostly textiles or food. He once designed a dryer for Special K cereal. I am sure he liked what he did, but his real love, woodworking, consumed his free time.

The supporting pillars of our cellar divided the basement into a woodworking shop on one side and a play area on the other. The shop was neat and orderly. Two roomy cabinets on either side of a long, three-inch-thick workbench housed tools of every description. Hand saws, drills, hammers, screwdrivers, clamps, chisels, and planes in multiple sizes hung in descending order.

A bank of drawers at the back of the workbench held a variety of nails, screws, router bits, protective glasses, gloves, and a multitude of other items that my dad considered necessary for his hobby.

Paint cans of varying sizes and brushes, large and small, always cleaned after use, were stored at the far end of the cellar atop an old desk. The strong odor of turpentine permeated this area. Squares of gold-leaf paper, hidden from view in a desk drawer, intrigued me. I liked to examine this collection of shiny papers, being careful not to have them disintegrate in my hands. Sometimes I wondered if all that gold was an indication of some hidden wealth.

The large, heavy drawer under the workbench held more pocket knives than any one person would ever need. This was the only disorderly spot in the workshop.

I had permission to use the free-standing drill-press anytime without asking. A fat slab of wood became the recipient of dozens of holes. It resembled a chunk of Swiss cheese by the time I had completed my drilling. I never created anything useful, but it was fun, and I am sure being busy kept me out of my father's way.

The huge circular band saw remained off limits to everyone but my dad. It made a sound so deafening you could hear it outside. Dad once cut off the tip of his right thumb using this machine. In his panic, he opened the door of the furnace and tossed the partially severed appendage into the fire. Mom said he must have been in shock and the thumb tip probably could have been re-attached if he had saved it. As kids we had a fascination with my dad's shortened thumb and sometimes examined this interesting stub up close.

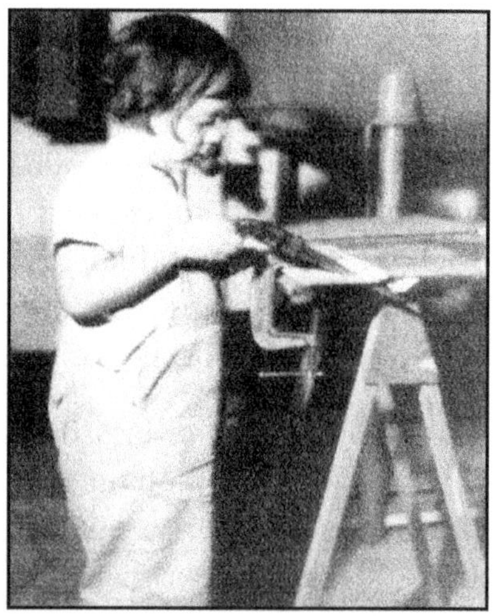

Three-year-old Alicia working on a project

My father gave us permission to use his hand saws and hammers anytime, but only if we promised to return them to their proper spot afterwards. We never abused this privilege, since we knew our dad would be true to his word.

After he completed a project, we heard the unmistakable rumble of his homemade shop vacuum that he fashioned out of a metal trash can. Hearing the roar, Mary, Alicia, and I scrambled down the cellar stairs all the while yelling, *"STOP, DAD, STOP!"* Scurrying about, we

I received a blue painted cradle and Mary a pink one made by our dad

gathered the curly shavings of planed scraps off the cellar floor and pressed the long, bouncy, wood curls into our hair. When satisfied with our new look, we ran upstairs holding on to our new tresses. My mother always enjoyed our impromptu fashion shows.

My father took pleasure in working with a wide variety of materials and woods. I am sure we had the only polished stainless-steel mailbox and five-foot tall pyramid-shaped incinerator in our town. He designed a form to make two cement planters for our front entrance. They were so heavy that they remain in the same spot today as they did all those many years ago.

He constructed benches and a table that fit perfectly into our breakfast nook. For many years he concentrated on making replicas of stately, formal, Eli Terry clocks. Most were made from mahogany, a favorite material. Roman numerals, painted on with a steady hand, were the lettering of choice on the clock face. When that tedious, exacting job was complete, Mary, the artistic one in the family, painted delicate roses in all four corners.

Dad made a play area for us in the backyard. I remember a sandbox, filled with dirt, not sand; a wooden dandle (A dandle is a see-saw. This usage is unique to the Narragansett Bay area); and a rope swing with a wooden seat attached to the Norway maple tree. He built several pieces of yard furniture. The hefty Adirondack chairs were almost impossible to move or extricate yourself from, but the canvas and wood sway-back lounge seats were comfortable and fun to sit in.

I had two favorite things that my father made. A secret stair going to the second floor lifted up on two hinges and never failed to grab my attention. Our family used this dark storage area for rain footgear. Sometimes I took every boot and rubber out, but I could never get my hand to reach the seemingly bottomless repository. I wondered what was down there at the very base of this ominous, mysterious, place. A flashlight, had I thought of it, would have revealed the secret of this perplexing storage spot.

The mahogany automatic cigarette dispenser ranks as the number one favorite gadget. As children we spent many hours

Me having fun on our backyard dandle

playing with this intriguing boxy contraption that made cigarettes appear, as if by magic, one by one, nestled in a slot cut into a small sliding drawer. This was offered to guests to have a smoke and maybe my mother used this device to retrieve the one cigarette a year she indulged in on her birthday.

One unsuccessful piece of furniture was a side-by-side double desk dad made for Mary and me. The oversized, forest green, handsome

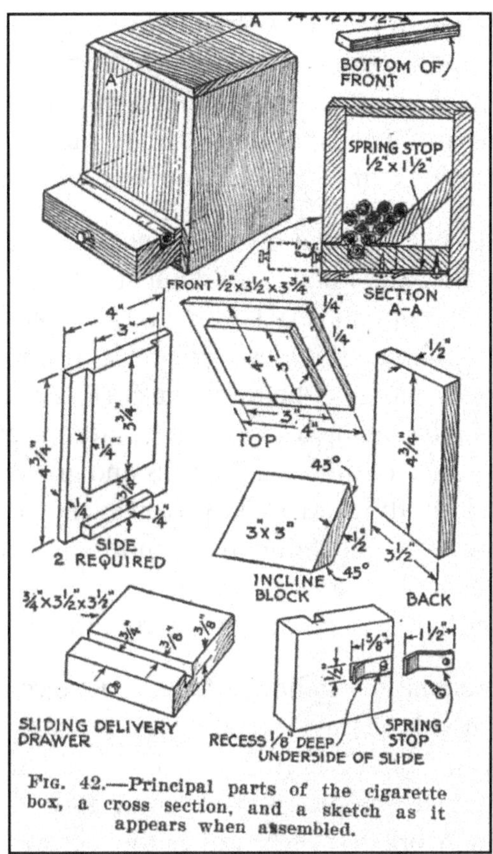

Fig. 42.—Principal parts of the cigarette box, a cross section, and a sketch as it appears when assembled.

The Home Workshop Manual that my father used to make many of his creations, including the cigarette dispenser box

art deco rectangular study table did not work. We sat side by side elbowing each other, while pushing our homework back and forth for being "on my half." This short-lived item quietly vanished down to the cellar. Mary went back to doing her homework stretched out on her bed and I used an antique, birdseye maple desk in the hall.

I knew at age thirteen I had to have a vanity in my bedroom and requested one, hoping my father would build it for me. He disappeared into the cellar and, within a week, carried a completed vanity up to our second-floor bedroom. I did notice a slight familiarity to the vanquished double desk.

For my birthday I received a three-way, stand-up mirror that I found advertised in the Sears catalog. The mirror and the new vanity were a perfect fit. I spent considerable lengths of time fashioning and re-fashioning my hair, applying various shades of lipstick, and sometimes just staring at my teenage face from three different angles.

My father said I needed a vanity chair, not the one from my desk. I watched as he sliced his band saw almost through the width of a piece of thick cherry wood every half inch. He soaked the wood for a few days in the bathtub until it was pliable. Using considerable force, with the aid of vices and glue, he formed a perfect circle and attached three legs. The round seat, upholstered in a pale, apricot brocade, was beautiful. The whole ensemble, glamorous and grown-up, resembled something from a Hollywood movie. However, the chair did have a serious flaw: three legs. It fell over countless times with me on it. Three legs did not work, but I never asked my dad to put on a fourth. I soon became proficient at balancing on my three-legged chair.

Following retirement my father devoted time to rebuilding antique clocks. Twice a month he traveled into Providence to a small antique shop at the foot of College Hill that specialized only in clocks. He brought the damaged timepieces back home to be reconstructed in his well-equipped workshop. My father took great pleasure in this exacting, technical, specialized craft.

Our "Jonathan Jo" continued to be engaged in his favorite pastime until a few weeks prior to his death.

I kept the tradition of reading the poetry of A.A. Milne to my children and then to my grandchildren, including that favorite of long ago, "Jonathan Jo."

IN VOGUE

A McQuiggan Outfit

This McQuiggen* outfit was made from fabric that felt good. I liked to run my fingers across the narrow grey and peach raised, bumpy, diagonal stripes set against a white background. That remained its only redeeming feature.

I remember walking to school wearing this "new" dress feeling melancholy. The wide ruffle at the hem skimmed the top of my socks. The heavy, cotton, woven fabric caused everything to droop. I recall being directly in front of Dr. Blake's dental office and reflecting on something that had never entered my mind before.

I feel poor.

I feel poor wearing this dress.

My mother sewed for us all the time, but I do not remember her adjusting McQuiggen clothes. She must have known the hem needed work, but taking up a ruffle was a major sewing job. I guess she just ignored it.

I was embarrassed at recess in this floppy, too-long, dress. I decided to not wear it again, but I did, and I felt no different than the first time.

I had learned my lesson and never put it on it again.

**McQuiggen clothes: clothes sent to us from a family friend who had two daughters with an abundance of mostly nice clothes.*

THREADS

Second Chance

"The mailman just dropped off a McQuiggan box," my mother shouted as she stood in the living room holding a sizable package.

Mary and I did not need a second summons. We came charging down from upstairs, pushing and shoving to get there first to rip open the unexpected parcel.

The McQuiggans lived in New Jersey but I think Jimmy, their father, had been a neighbor to the Maguires in Rumford growing up. They mailed us a box brimming with stylish clothes about three times a year.

They had two daughters a little older than Mary and me. We didn't need the clothes, but it was a thoughtful gesture that some families did in those days.

Some of my very favorite outfits that I ever owned came from the McQuiggans, but there were some clothes that were never worn, or even worse, brought bad luck, like my stunning satin underpants.

Mary often wore a handsome pair of brown, twill McQuiggin jodhpurs with genuine leather suede leg protectors. The sides of the pants flared out and form-fitting fabric around her calves and ankles gave the appearance of an official riding outfit. A stranger might even have thought she owned a horse.

One time I grabbed a small pigskin clutch bag. It was covered with minute depressions over the entire surface. I was sure that each little void had once held a pig hair. Mary thought it looked disgusting, but I liked my intriguing, strange-looking purse and wore it on special occasions.

Our most desired clothing of all were several gowns that were most likely worn at school dances. We strolled around the backyard in our fancy outfits and sometimes posed for pictures in the flower garden next door. My favorite was a pink organdy ruffled ensemble trimmed with black velvet ribbon. I also loved the sheer, elegant, soft violet gown constructed with wide, puffy, long sleeves. This gossamer, dramatic floor-length gown reminded me of an evening dress Greer Garson might have worn in a romantic movie. We were lucky enough to have two sources of these hand-me-down gowns. Some were given to us by Loretta McDougal, my Aunt Kay and Uncle Bill's

My friend, Doreen, and I model gowns in 1950

niece, who had a beautiful voice and wore these fancy outfits while performing at local talent recitals.

Once I spotted a pair of bunny-fur mittens in the box.

"They're mine," I yelled, before Mary had the opportunity to utter a single syllable.

I loved anything bunny fur. I put them on. They were a perfect fit. Each mitten had soft, fluffy fur on the top with bright, kelly green leather palms on the underside.

These mittens, resembling ones that so many of my friends had received for Christmas, were not quite up to standard. Everyone I knew had red leather palms on their mittens, not green. I was disappointed,

106

but I thought if I kept the green side down no one would notice. A more serious and noticeable flaw loomed larger than the green palms and it made me want to reconsider ownership. The bunny fur, over the years, had yellowed. I could hide the green from view, but not the yellow. I put both mittens on and walked over to the front window.

"Yellow," I muttered in disappointment.

"Mary, you can have these mittens. I'll trade you them for that red pocketbook."

"Nope. You grabbed the mittens first and now they are yours."

Mary had a flair for style. Even as a young person her eye for fashion was keen and she knew, without a second glance, I had chosen the wrong thing and she would not be caught wearing off-color bunny-fur mittens.

My mother, who had a tonic for just about everything, spoke up.

"Anita, go find a shoebox in my closet. Get the cornmeal from the pantry and sprinkle some in the bottom of the box. Put the mittens in and shake a fair amount over all the bunny fur. Cornmeal, I heard, will whiten yellowed fur."

"How did she know this? Did she make it up? Did she find this information in some woman's magazine?"

As cock-eyed and bizarre as this all seemed, I was willing to give my mother's home remedy a try.

I had serious doubts about this anticipated miraculous transformation. I poured cornmeal over the mittens and placed the cover on the shoebox, then slipped it under a neat stack of ironed sheets in the linen closet and waited for a blessed metamorphosis.

All spring I checked the box on a regular basis, but nothing seemed to happen. Sometimes I shook the box without glancing inside, hoping to be surprised by the next viewing. As fall began to usher in the winter months, I turned the mittens over, sometimes daily, like a short-order cook flipping pancakes on a griddle. Time was of the essence. Strangely, I never lost faith that the promise of sparkling, white, bunny-fur mittens was only a shake away.

A new dire set of circumstances arose. The cornmeal began to cling to the fur. I shook the mittens. I stroked the bunny fur as if it was the family pet. This caused friction and resulted in the cornmeal adhering with greater resolve. I wore the mittens anyway, hiding the unstylish green palms while discretely picking out cornmeal as it came to the surface, hoping that my friends did not notice my fashion faux pas.

This secret passion for anything with white bunny fur did not abate. A pair of much-anticipated earmuffs never appeared in any of the future McQuiggan boxes. I think every girl in my fifth-grade class owned this stylish headgear but me. I asked for them one Christmas and I did receive earmuffs that year, but not the sparkling, fluffy, white ones I longed for.

"Thanks, Mom. Thanks, Dad," trying hard to mask my letdown.

There they were, two enormous thick mounds of compacted genuine lamb's wool earmuffs, looking like two scoops of vanilla ice cream attached to each ear. A bluish steel band connected the offending earmuffs. I tried them on. The metal clasp pressed against my head with the intensity of a carpenter's wood vise. I could see everyone's lips moving in conversation, but the dense, sheered wool connected to thick impenetrable animal hide prevented me from hearing anything that was being said.

"Anita, you know that lamb's wool will last forever, and they will be much warmer than bunny fur."

Sometimes my mother was just too sensible, level headed, and practical. She knew how long I babied those bunny-fur mittens. Wouldn't it just follow that earmuffs, the right kind, would be the perfect Christmas gift for me?

I did wear my bulbous, off-white earmuffs and they did keep my ears warm. They were of such high quality that they never wore out, but my friends did tire of me saying time after time, "Huh, what did you say? I can't hear you."

· · · · ·

A few years ago, I visited my sisters, Mary and Alicia, in Boston. They had read in the newspaper that the longstanding Foxboro Hat Company was liquidating the store's merchandise and closing its doors forever. That was familiar territory since we always made a stop at this favorite hat store en route to Boston for a shopping trip to Filene's Basement.

The hat store was located at the top of a steep, narrow stairway on the second floor of a wooden clapboard building in the old section of Foxboro that must have been at one time the business center of this former manufacturing hub.

I remembered some hats were in deep drawers. Others were displayed on flat wooden discs supported by elegant footed dowels. We loved to try on whatever met our fancy, especially the wide-brim straw hats festooned with profusions of colorful spring flowers. You could try on as many hats as you desired without the interruption of a sales clerk. That is what made it so much fun. The hats looked sophisticated and fashionable and made me think that any millinery shop in New York City would look no different.

On this particular day, Mary, Alicia, and I climbed the worn, wooden stairs, chatting away and lamenting the store's closing. Hats were everywhere in disarray. There were odd things like inexpensive vests and men's jackets that were foreign to a hat shop. It was disappointing, but we were not deterred and set off in different directions, hoping to find a bargain. We were there only a short time when I heard my sister beckon in a muffled voice.

"Nita, Nita, come quick. Look what I found," Alicia called from an adjoining room. I found her bent over leaning into an enormous cardboard box. She pulled out something white.

"Look at this. It is perfect for Anne. It's just adorable."

Anne was my four-year-old granddaughter who liked pretty things. It wasn't earmuffs or mittens, but a beautiful, dazzlingly white bunny-fur child's muff. The fur was flat from being at the bottom of the box under a vast array of merchandise, just waiting to be discovered.

I held the muff and brought it up to my face. I blew at the spotless white fluff. The fur separated and danced with each breath.

"Try it on," Alicia insisted.

I put the woven rayon cord over my head, with the muff reaching chest high. I squeezed one hand into it and felt the smooth, cool satin lining against my skin.

"You have to get it. It is only seven dollars. I know how you love bunny fur." Alicia insisted. "Anne will adore it."

I made the only purchase that day at the soon-to-be extinct Foxboro Hat Company.

I gave Anne the child-sized muff the following Christmas. She put the cord over her head, slipped her hands into the muff and lifted it up to her beautiful, young face. She rubbed the fur gently against her cheek and, for a moment, closed her eyes and rocked her body gently enjoying the moment.

"Thank you, Grandma. It's nice and soft."

I never saw Anne wear it after that one time on Christmas day, but that was allright. I knew when I purchased that fluffy, white, perfect bunny-fur muff it was not really intended for my little granddaughter.

JIMMY-THE-TRAMP

An Onion to Go

The rapping and incessant banging on the back door could be heard from every room of my grandmother's house.

She knew who it was even before opening the door.

"I'm coming. I'm coming," she yelled as she clambered down the stairs from her second floor sewing room.

He stood at the door grinning, appearing a bit thinner than last year, in his all-too-large work overalls.

"Hello, Jimmy, it is good to see you. I have plenty of chores to keep you busy for a couple of days," said my grandmother.

"Hello, Miss Maguire, I'm ready to work."

My mother told me about this man and always referred to him as Jimmy-the-Tramp. He appeared in the neighborhood as regular as clockwork come the first warm spring day. He seemed to materialize out of nowhere, but once the cooler weather approached, he left as quickly as he came. He never mentioned where he vanished to during the winter months.

"Well, Jimmy, there is plenty of wood out near the shed to be chopped for the kitchen stove and the furnace. The windows need a thorough cleaning and the lilacs have just gotten out of control and could use a good trim."

Jimmy obliged and started his assigned tasks. Around supper my grandmother gave him a nice hot meal and, more often than not, he asked if he could sleep in the cellar for the night. She provided some blankets and Jimmy settled in on the floor by the furnace.

Rising early, he completed his jobs and again appeared at the back door.

"Anything else, Miss Maguire?"

"No, I think you have finished about all that needs to be done."

She paid him but, before leaving, he always had one final request.

"Miss Maguire, can I have an onion for the road?"

My grandmother walked over to the vegetable bin, picked out a big yellow onion, and handed it to Jimmy.

He continued going from house to house around the neighborhood looking for work. My mother told me he did not say much but, when he did, he often reminded his customers,

"I never want to be buried in Potter's Field. No, sir, that is something that I don't want ever to happen to me."

One summer, my mother told me Jimmy died while working at a neighbor's home. Everyone remembered his wish and a collection was taken up among the neighbors to give him a proper interment in Rumford's only cemetery.

I wish I had asked my mother his whole name, but my guess is that as a young girl, she only referred to this gentle soul as Jimmy-the-Tramp.

I would have liked to visit his grave and place a bouquet of spring flowers and maybe an onion, if only I had known just a little more about Jimmy-the-Tramp.

ILL WIND

Surviving Hurricane Carol, 1954

"Hail Mary full of grace, the Lord is with thee…"

My mother and Aunt Esther are silently praying the rosary. Both are staring straight ahead, as fingers move along the beads of the rosaries tucked in the front folds of their dresses. Normally, they would be chatting and laughing, but we are riding through a hurricane that is raging along the southern New England shoreline.

We departed Grand Central Station a short time ago and are en route to Union Station in Providence. The train struggles along at a snail's pace. This intense storm, coming in off the Atlantic Ocean along the Connecticut shore, has put us all in harm's way. It is August 31, 1954.

My sister, Mary, and I are across the aisle in the almost empty railroad car, kneeling on the seats with our faces pressed against the cool window. The rain is so intense and coming down with such force, that it partially obstructs our view. As we strain to see what is taking place outside, the wind momentarily shifts. The fury of the hurricane winds causes the waves to dash against the bottom rim of our railroad car in bursts, sounding like the low reverberation of a base drum. Our window vibrates. For a moment we can see outside. The waves appear angry and devoid of any rhythmic pattern. The sea is the color of ink as it rolls and heaves. From our vantage point it appears as if the train is riding atop the water.

"Get away from the windows, girls."

We reluctantly obey our mother's directive and do as we are told. The adults appear stone-faced. Their praying continues. Mary and I are bored, cold, and hungry.

We rose very early on this late summer morning to travel on a one-day trip to New York City. My dad drove us to Union Station to catch the first train out.

My mother's first cousin, Harry Obert, and his wife, Betty, from Erie, Pennsylvania, are taking an ocean voyage to Europe on the *SS Mauritania*. Their only child, Bob, had been to Europe the year before and they are retracing his journey.

Our cousin Bob, a handsome, talented, personable young man, about to enter his second year at Cornell, was killed, along with his Aunt Florence, in an automobile accident on their way to Chautauqua, New York, over a year ago.

Florence was a favorite cousin, too. She taught first grade in Erie and was an expert on birds. Florence often came to my grandmother's during the summertime for a lengthy visit. She paid attention to Mary and me and allowed us to play hairdresser, styling her pretty, wavy, premature grey hair for as long as it held our interest.

A year later the loss of these beloved cousins remains. Going to New York affords us an opportunity to show Harry and Betty our enduring love for Florence and Bob.

We enjoy the train ride to Grand Central Station and hail a cab that takes us to the piers on the East River. The driver lets us off within view of the *SS Mauritania*. It is massive. I have never seen a passenger ship before. We walk up the steep gangway, clutching the guard rail, trying to avoid a glance at the swirling water far below.

We weave our way through narrow corridors to Harry and Betty's stateroom. Mary and I expected something luxurious, resembling the pictures in ads taken from the pages of *Holiday* magazine. We are disappointed. The tiny, cramped, almost suffocating, room has bunk beds, a table, two chairs, and a compact bathroom. The porthole offered reassurance that their stateroom was above the waterline.

All adults, except my Aunt Esther, enjoy some champagne. Betty draws our attention to an enormous wicker basket brimming with fruit, chocolates, cookies, and nuts that someone has sent to them. She encourages Mary and me to help ourselves to whatever we would like. We get *the look* from my mother and know what it means. We each take an orange.

An announcement crackles over the loudspeaker. We can barely make out what is being said.

"All who are not registered passengers on the *SS Mauritania* must leave the ship now."

We kiss them goodbye and quickly depart. Once outside, Mary and I toss the confetti bought for the occasion and wave to all sea-bound travelers that are calling out to friends and family as they press against the ship's railings. Standing on the wooden pier, we watch as the *SS Mauritania* departs, stern first, from her mooring. She maneuvers in reverse with the precision of an elephant backing out of its stall. She turns in the channel and proceeds down the East River.

There is no time to linger if we are to catch the late afternoon train back to Providence.

Our cab lets us off at the main doors of Grand Central station.

Once on the train, we all enjoy the oranges. They taste good. Mary exclaims that she thinks we should have taken some chocolates. Even Aunt Es and my mother agree.

As we leave New York it begins to rain. The conductor informs us there is a hurricane along the coast and it will delay our arrival time into Providence. The rain is now unrelenting as we approach Connecticut. The train slows down and soon comes to a jarring stop. The sudden lurch throws us all forward, then backward but, within a few minutes, we are on our way again and the train lumbers along like an old dog mile after mile.

The conductor yells, "Old Saybrook, Old Saybrook."

The train jerks back and forth then screeches to a grinding stop. A few men with briefcases head out into the storm.

We get underway again and the train moves so slowly that I imagine the distance can be measured in inches. The winds begin to pick up and our car rocks from one side to the other, as if searching for its equilibrium. I think Aunt Esther and my mother, after chatting for a while in low whispers, have gone back to praying.

Mary and I shift in our seats attempting to sleep. It does not come, so we talk. We are both afraid and wonder if the ground supporting the iron rails is in danger of being washed away. Our railroad car is now dark. Occasionally the conductor walks through with a flashlight checking the occupants.

Hours go by and the train's stop-and-go journey takes its toll on Mary and me. We begin to push each other, concerning who is hogging the seat. Mary gets up and settles in across the aisle.

Hours pass. We notice that the wind is beginning to abate, but it is still raining. The wide swing the train makes as it approaches Providence is familiar, since we have taken the New York trip several times to visit my Aunt Alice and Uncle Con.

The conductor comes through our car yelling,

"Providence, Providence. Next stop, Providence."

We all sit up straight and strain our eyes in hopes of spotting the Providence skyline. We can see nothing. The city is in total darkness. The train creaks and groans and again begins to rock from side to side. For a moment it feels like we are going to tip completely over.

No one is talking and I am pushing my body forward foolishly thinking this may help us get to our destination sooner. The train comes to an abrupt stop and it is time for us to depart our cold and dark railroad car.

"Providence. Providence. Watch your step, young lady."

The conductor warns us to be careful as we descend the metal steps on to the platform. He then escorts all the departing passengers into Union Station with his flashlight.

The cavernous lobby is in semi-darkness with a few emergency lights casting an eerie glow throughout the room. We are a tight little group walking together looking for my father, who may not have made it into the city. My mother breaks away and dashes toward a familiar figure standing directly under the ceiling dome. Now we all hurry to greet him. It's my dad!

Our car is parked directly in front of the entrance door. We all must take a giant step to enter the car since the water is halfway up the hubcaps. Dad avoids the usual route home along the Providence River, but turns to high ground: up College Hill, by Brown University and across the Red Bridge. He drives along the outskirts of Rumford, through East Providence, and then on to Riverside. We weave around fallen trees and avoid washed-out streets and sagging wires. This is the second trip for my dad into Providence to meet up with us on this wild night. It is a harrowing ride. The lights of our car cast long, ghostly, shadows along the empty roadways.

We enter our driveway and notice our favorite, umbrella-shaped Norway maple in our backyard has fallen victim to the storm. By now the rain and wind have stopped.

Alicia has been staying with the Overdeep family across the street and when they see our car headlights they escort my little sister home. She is frightened, yet happy to see her family intact and begins to cry.

We tell Alicia that Harry and Betty left on their sentimental journey sailing to Europe to honor Bob and Florence but we, too, embarked on an unexpected adventure of our own. We spent fourteen long hours on the train: a normal four-hour ride.

I explained to Alicia, "We were cold, hungry, scared, and bored, but that doesn't matter now because we are all home safely, and guess what? Aunt Es has promised to visit with us for a few days."

*On August 31, 1954, Hurricane Carol made her way up the southern New England coast. There were 72 fatalities. The storm destroyed almost 4,000 homes, 3,500 automobiles, and 3,000 boats. All of Rhode Island lost electrical power. Parts of Providence were under twelve feet of water. Block Island recorded the strongest gust of wind ever at 135 mph. The Connecticut shoreline experienced storm surges from five to fifteen feet of water. The storm came in at high tide. Hurricane Carol was so deadly, her name was retired.**

**Southern New England Tropical Storms and Hurricanes, by David R. Vallee and Michael R. Dion. National Weather Service, Taunton, MA.*

*Storm surge from Hurricane Carol lashes the Edgewood Yacht
Club near the southern end of Rhode Island toward
the Connecticut shoreline on August 31, 1954
Source: NOAA Photo Library from Wikimedia Commons*

ROYAL TREATMENT
Winter Respite

Two days off from school in mid-February was routine for me. Sometimes I did have a sinus infection but, more often, I pretended to be sick. I knew good things were in my immediate future.

Being sick at my house was the stuff dreams were made of. It bordered on spa treatment, Riverside style. My day or days at home, without cause, followed a predictable, comforting routine.

"Anita, you go in and take a bath and brush your teeth while I fix up your room. Your breakfast is on the kitchen table."

Readying my room always took more time than I expected, so I sat on a dining room chair wearing my favorite blue wool robe with matching slippers and waited.

My mother soon appeared carrying a bundle of wrinkled bedding ready to be washed. I climbed the stairs to the second floor knowing my room was now all set for the sick child.

I opened the bedroom door, bracing my body for a cold blast. My mother always opened the two windows right to the top to air everything out while she busied herself tidying up my room. The crisp air felt refreshing.

She soon returned with a comb and brush and untangled my long braids. She then parted my hair down the middle and styled it again in pigtails (braids).

"Ah, you look nice, Anita. I will be back upstairs very soon to read you *Snip, Snap, and Snurr.*"

I loved the stories of those fair-headed, young identical triplets dressed in matching shorts, shirts, and shoes with button closures. Their mundane lives in faraway Sweden evolved into grand adventures for my young imagination.

I knew what to expect when I entered my aired-out, cold bedroom, yet somehow it always surprised me, like opening a birthday gift when you knew the contents. I could smell the clean, laundry-fresh aroma of the spotless, ironed cotton sheets. I did not need to peer under the blanket to see that the corners of the bed 'linen' had precise enveloped corners. My two pillows, fluffed and covered with smooth cases, were trimmed with a single row of tatting crafted by my mother. A plethora of comforts invited me to lay back and relax. I climbed into bed and drew the covers up under my chin to ward off the chill.

The night table beside my bed held a few things, like the Chinese puzzle, Chen Yen, given to us by my father and brought out only for the special occasion of recuperation when one of us was sick. My favorite books and a drawing pad and pencil on the night table were close at hand. The most anticipated item on the stand glistened and fizzed in a glass. The morning sun, coming through the southeast facing windows made the contents of the tall tumbler sparkle. I watched the bubbles climb to the rim of the glass and shoot into the air like the spray from a miniature garden hose. The golden hue of the White Rock dry ginger ale caused me to salivate. I checked to see if the tall container held the bent glass straw or the straight one. The straw with the slight curve, the favored one, allowed me to lean back on my pillows and daydream, gazing out the windows watching the branches of the Norway maple sway in the breeze as I sipped my effervescent tonic. In our household, soda, like the Chinese puzzle, only appeared if you were ill.

I clicked open the clear, plastic case containing the black, white, and red geometric Chinese puzzle pieces and dumped its contents on my bed cover dreaming that I did not know the secret of putting them together. This compact game lay hidden under the table linens in the dining room buffet all year until one of us became ill. The puzzle whereabouts were not secret, but Mary, Alicia, and I did not play with it until the game appeared on our night table.

Following my cousin Alice's death, her doll cradle along with many of her other toys came to rest in the eaves of our attic. Periodically we would climb into the dim, shadowy storage area only to look at them. They were still hers, not ours. There was one exception to this rule. Mother went into the attic when we were sick and brought out a box that held many small, painted, wooden blocks that could be arranged in a variety of designs. We took great care manipulating the pieces, but being on guard so as not to make the mistake of sitting on the box cover and flattening it.

When my father was not on an out-of-state job, I could count on hearing his approaching footsteps before he announced his arrival at the top of the stairs. He placed my evening meal on an aqua tray that he had made for us and decorated with yellow daffodil decals. The main function was a serving tray, but the top tilted in such a way that we could also use it for writing or drawing.

He placed a bowl of steamy hot milk toast on the tray. This well-loved concoction, in my mother's best, pink china, smelled buttery and looked inviting. A soup spoon rested on a large white napkin.

I loved the special attention he gave me. The simple meal my dad created just for me dissolved in my mouth and slid, warm and gentle, on its downward healing journey.

My father cooked two things: paper thin, egg-rich crepe suzettes rolled-up like a jelly roll with a liberal serving of strawberry jam tucked inside and a bit of powdered sugar on top, and the satisfying hot milk toast which he made only when we were sick. The crepes made an occasional appearance for breakfast or Sunday night supper.

As the day wore on, I tired of games, books, and drawing pictures. I leaned back and clicked on the radio. My father never liked the original case of our radio, so he constructed a new wooden one made from maple that he polished to a smooth-to-the-touch satin patina. We did not have good reception on the second floor. It was necessary to press a long, tangled copper wire protruding from the back of the radio with your index finger and thumb. I found it tiring and frustrating listening to music fading in and out as my finger began to ache. My mind drifted and I wondered what was going on at school and in the neighborhood. Night came slowly as I tossed and turned trying to sleep. I drifted off listening to the comforting moan of the fog horn in the distance, wondering if tomorrow would be the day I announced to my mother that I had recovered.

Just the other day I called my sister, Alicia, and asked, "Do you remember how special things were for us when we were sick as kids?"

"Do I?" she immediately responded.

"Oh, those sheets! Were they linen?"

"No Alicia, we didn't have linen sheets, but they were very good cotton ones."

Alicia and I talked a few minutes and her remembrances of our royal treatment mostly matched mine.

My two young granddaughters, Molly and Bridget, had an overnight with me this past weekend. Bridget followed me into my bedroom.

"Grandma, your bedroom is always cold. How come?"

"You know when I was close to your age my mother would come up to my bedroom when I was sick and push open the windows to air out the room while she put fresh sheets on the bed. Being in a cold bedroom felt good to me back then so many, many years ago and it still does today. That's just the way Grandma likes it."

THE JEWEL THIEF

No Shame

I shook it once, and then a second time. It had been decades, but I knew in that very instant what the hollow of my childhood doll's belly contained. There, somewhere in the blackness of her torso, lay hidden a bracelet I stole from my sister, Mary, as a young child.

I engaged in borrowing, but my method was very different from drawing up a contract with a financial institution. My scheming approach was always minus permission from the owner.

As I grew older, I borrowed Mary's tasteful clothes without her knowledge. Borrowing was one thing, but stealing raised my petty crimes to an entirely different level.

For some reason, on this quiet, winter afternoon, I wanted to organize the few dolls I had remaining from my childhood. They were all in a large paper bag at the bottom of my old toy chest that my father made. The first one I pulled out was my bride doll. There she was in the bag stark naked, with the white taffeta wedding outfit my mother had sewed for her, wrinkled and appearing a bit discolored. Her blond wig, matted and askew on her head, made this once regal doll appear comical. I placed her eighteen-inch unclothed body on my bed. I jiggled her again.

The bracelet was not the only thing in my life I took without permission. I stared out the window of my bedroom and began to daydream of times past.

One Christmas Mary received an ankle-length, flannel, blue-and-white checked nightgown, flowing with yards of fabric. It featured a deep ruffle along the entire hem and around both wrists. A wide, satin, sky-blue neckline bow cascaded down almost the entire length of the garment making you think that once upon a time it belonged to a princess.

The handsome sleep apparel had been purchased by my mother on a sale rack at one of the better department stores in Providence. It did not get folded in Mary's dresser drawer along with her lesser assortment of nightwear, but she hung it on a hanger on her side of our closet.

When Mary had an overnight invitation at one of her girlfriend's homes, I waited like a fox stalking its prey anticipating her departure. She never took that dreamy, bulky nightgown on these teenage adventures since it required most of the space in her small, trendy, blue plaid, zippered hatbox. I waited out of sight for her to slam the back door. I dashed up to our closet, two stairs at a time, donned the coveted nightgown, then pranced around our bedroom admiring myself in my new Sears three-way mirror propped on the vanity. The nightgown felt soft and luxurious.

I yelled goodnight to my parents from the top of the stairs and climbed into bed, adorned in an ocean of soft blue and white flannel. Mary never discovered the many times I wore this lovely article of clothing in her absence.

Life did not stay so simple and innocent. Mary caught me several times wearing one of her blouses or skirts. When I attended Riverside Junior High, she began to check the contents of her closet when she arrived home from high school earlier in the afternoon.

One day she asked to see my junior high group graduation picture. I had not mentioned that it had arrived in the mail, but somehow she knew. There I was squinting in the late afternoon sun with all my classmates outside the school building, standing shoulder to shoulder with my best friends, Nancy and Sue. I wore my perfectly ironed, cotton, tangerine circle skirt, and a white Ship n' Shore blouse sporting its signature Peter Pan collar. A delicate flower pin attached to the collar completed the ensemble. Mary ran her finger painstakingly slow along each row of students until she found me.

Riverside Junior High ninth grade graduation

At first, she said nothing. I held my breath.

Her eyes narrowed. I tensed, awaiting her reaction. In a controlled, low, steady, chilling voice she exclaimed,

"That is MY flower pin."

She let the picture drop to the table and walked off. I wished she had carried on and yelled at me or even told our mother. She, like me, could have predicted our mother's familiar phrase:

"You two handle it."

I suddenly realized I had been staring out the window daydreaming for some time.

I picked up my bride doll, shook her again, then pulled down on her left leg. It came off in my hand. The other leg quickly followed along with two rotten rubber bands tumbling out of the small cavity. I held her up by her arms and they, too, parted from her upper body. The stolen bracelet slipped out through a leg opening and on to the bedspread. To my horror, her head tipped back and rolled off to join the appendages. Her striking light-blue eyes looked at me one last time and then closed shut. I stared at my dismembered doll for a moment, gathered up her parts, placed everything back in the paper bag and carried them over to the toy chest. I shut the lid, went back into the bedroom, and put the very tiny brass bracelet in a safe place.

A few days later I went to locate the stolen item, but I could not find it.

Had I vacuumed it up? Did it get lost in an article of clothing? I was mystified.

I walked over to the telephone and called the familiar Boston phone number. Mary answered. I told her my regrettable tale of childhood thievery. She showed no sympathy for my now-dismembered bride doll or any forgiveness for my errant behavior. It was as if I had opened up an old wound. Mary had no recollection of ever having owned this small, doll-sized bracelet, but that did not seem to matter.

"Well, where do you think you put my bracelet? I wonder if it is valuable? What, you lost it so soon?"

"Mary, it resembled a prize you might find hidden in a box of Cracker Jacks."

"I don't care. I would like to see it. Then I might remember. Call me when you find it."

It was as if we were kids again: squabbling over nothing.

"Okay. Okay. I will. Got to run. The timer just went off on the stove."

"Don't forget. Call me. Believe me, I do remember. You were really bad sometimes."

IN VOGUE

All Clothes Are Not Created Equal

My mother sewed this hated outfit as a Christmas dress when I was in the ninth grade.

This not-quite-holiday-red dress incorporated all my fashion dislikes:

- Collar: mock design with two points rather than a normal, around-the-neck collar.

- Skirt: the dreaded, matronly, semi-flared skirt making it look as if my mom ran out of fabric.

- Color: a hint of orange in the red.

- Belt: a way-too-narrow belt not unlike those worn by zoot suiters*.

The single saving grace of this holiday frock had to be a later addition: shiny gold buttons down the front that served as decoration only.

I never told my mother that I really didn't like this dress. I did not want to hurt her feelings. She thought I looked lovely in this holiday frock. I wore it a lot.

*Zoot suiters: boys who wore suit jackets with squared-off, pointy shoulders and narrow, pegged-in pant legs. The pants were held up using a skinny belt with the buckle angled to one side. Shiny, shapeless, dark gabardine seemed to be the fabric of choice. A zoot suiter wanted to date me in high school. He was actually a nice kid, but with bad taste in clothes.

PAX

Shuffling the Cards

Several prayer cards were scattered on a small, mahogany table at the entrance to the church. I picked one up and slipped it into my coat pocket. I had arrived for my friend, Carol's, funeral. I felt so sad and grief-stricken, that I didn't care if I ever read it.

Prayer cards have been in my life for as far back as I can remember. Now, at my age, I find myself reluctantly beginning to amass a small collection.

In some ways I am just like my mother and my aunts, I thought. Their missals were the repository for dozens of these cards that recorded the birth and death of a deceased family member or a friend. Usually a colored picture of a saint adorned the front of the card with a brief prayer printed on the reverse side just below the deceased's vital statistics.

Following the deaths of my mother and my aunts, I received their prayer books. I don't know why my sisters handed them on to me, but they did. The books were black leather, mostly well-worn, and dog-eared from years of use. My aunts and my mother were women of firm religious beliefs who practiced their faith daily.

These impressive volumes, with gold letters and symbols stamped on the cover, were very different in appearance from the small, shiny, pastel-colored Mass prayer book I received when I made my First Communion. My book cover featured an image of a youthful Jesus reaching out to three young, Caucasian children. Most prayers were written in English with the left page in Latin.

As children, the cards we accumulated were known as holy cards, not prayer cards. They too had pictures and prayers on both sides, but without the message of someone's birth and death. These holy cards were often given as a reward for being a good student at St. Brendan's. You collected them like you would baseball cards.

The leather-bound books all told a story. My mother's prayer book held a cross-section of cards, reminders to pray for friends and relatives. Some of her cards were for people she barely knew, yet for some reason she considered them deserving of a few moments of her time.

My Aunt Esther's cards read like something out of a Dublin telephone book: Rooney, Reilly, Finn, Murphy, Maguire, Monahan, Cosgrove, Daly, and Doolin. Her prized card featured a handsome, young, forty-something man with a gentle smile. Under his photograph it read: John Fitzgerald Kennedy, 35th President of the United States, Born: May 29, 1917, Inaugurated: January 20, 1961, Died: November 22, 1963.

Aunt Alice's prayer book, puffy and misshapen, made me smile when I opened it. Many pages were transparent and oily, making reading difficult. Her book appeared as old as Archimedes' Ancient Book of Prayer.

Aunt Alice, being a New York City career girl, considered moisturizing cream taking on the same degree of importance as a first cup of morning coffee. Aunt Alice's soft and smooth hands transferred the oiliness on to the pages of her well-used prayer book.

Aunt Kay's prayer book was so thin that you wondered if it held any cards at all. Its slender appearance mirrored my aunt perfectly. She was neat, tidy, efficient, and often exuded a bit of mystery. She would never have considered carrying something bulbous or misshapen, taking on the appearance of an over-stuffed billfold. Outwardly her book looked new and unused, but it wasn't. As I turned the pages, I discovered cards of deceased priests, family members, and former teachers, like herself. A few slender pamphlets and unadorned cards with prayers, not reminders of death, but of life and promise, created a little collection tucked in against the rear cover. I felt sure these prayers and novenas, with gently worn edges, were in remembrance of her "Baby Alice."

When I was preparing to move to a smaller house, decisions needed to be made. I had too many books and lacked space to store them in my new home. All four prayer books had remained in my den bookcase, one stacked on top of the other for many years. I knew what I had to do. I opened each book, thought for a moment, retrieved the prayer cards, kissed each book, and then respectfully disposed of it. I took the card collection and placed it in the only prayer book I was keeping: my St. Joseph's Daily Missal that I purchased with my first teaching paycheck.

Winter was making its appearance and I walked into the front hall closet and reached for my warm coat. I put my hand in the pocket and pulled out Carol's long forgotten card. I read the little prayer. So much like Carol, I thought, all about the beauty of life and the joy of cultivating flower gardens. I walked into the living room and reached up to the top bookshelf to retrieve my missal. I opened it and placed her prayer card inside to join the others.

Friends

THE TOWNSEND GIRLS

Best Friends

The Townsend sisters, Rena, Nellie, Mary, and Florie, were always called the Townsend girls, even though they were grown women. These four sisters and their spouses remained my father's and mother's best friends all their adult lives.

Jack's graduation from Holy Cross College, 1953
(l-r) Nellie, Rena, Jack (Rena's son), Florie, Mary

They were the special people we invited to a surprise twenty-fifth wedding anniversary party for my parents. When my father died, they sat at the funeral parlor for both days of his wake. They did the same for my mother.

Mary, Alicia, and I saw these family friends often; Nellie more than the others, since she lived close by.

The Townsend girls were all small in stature with dainty hands and feet, fair skin, and they always wore makeup. They appeared soft and powdery, with heads of tiny curls and premature white hair. Florie and Nellie were not as stylish as Mary and Rena but, just the same, regularly visited the beauty parlor for permanents. I never saw them in anything other than dresses, but they did don casual clothes when we visited Rena's or Mary's summer homes in Touisset Point and Hope Valley.

These women were all married to men we looked forward to seeing as much as them.

All the Townsend girls had good Persian lamb coats. Some sported mink collars, others were plain. When they donned their ample winter coats that reached down to their ankles, they did not appear so tiny. Nellie, Rena, Mary, and Florie were thoughtful, kind, good, devout, and often funny women who loved a good laugh. Florie, though, had her moments.

Mary, Alicia, and I loved these wonderful ladies who brought such fun into our lives.

I know they loved us too.

Rena

Rena and my mother were best friends at East Providence High School. Mother said Rena was a beautiful girl in her teen years and that all the Townsend Girls were good looking when they were young. Rena remained attractive all her life.

She and her charming, dapper, gentleman husband, Al (Ratier), lived in the fishing and manufacturing town of Warren, Rhode Island, a few miles south of Riverside. Their spacious, old, white colonial house with black slat shutters was on tree-lined Washington Street, a pleasant walk to the center of town.

It intrigued me that their winter residence appeared not much different in size than their beach house at Touisset Point. The comfortable summer home, several miles south of Warren, was situated on a high embankment that overlooked a sandy beach on the Kickamuit River. I thought summer homes near the water were supposed to be cottage-like, small, with old furniture, and maybe smell musty. Their home did not.

Rena had a high-pitched voice and a musical laugh. When we arrived at the beach, the kitchen screen door swung open as soon as we turned into the driveway. Rena rushed out to greet us as if she had been waiting all day for our arrival.

A short distance out from the beach, a large, inviting diving platform, connected to the road by a bridge, remained our immediate objective upon our arrival at Touisset.

Rena and Al had two children, Joan and Jack, who were several years older than Mary and me and considerably older than Alicia.

Christmas at the Ratier's
Joan, me, Jack, Mary, and cousin Joyce Stockton

Joan, tall, pretty, with stunning eyes and thick, dark lashes, greeted us like favorite cousins. Her friendliness and attention to us never abated.

Jack, handsome, spoiled, and aloof, ignored us as best he could. A "Hi" typified his usual greeting and on a good day I would get "Hi, Nita." Jack had polio and wore heavy metal braces on both legs which required him to get around with the assistance of crutches. I remember him racing down the steep stairs of the embankment at Touisset Point using only his crutches and charging across the sand. At the water's edge he tossed his crutches behind him onto the sandy beach. He shot his upper body forward, landing in a shallow dive and swam, with lightening speed, out to the raft. We thought Jack to be mysterious and very appealing. Mary and I spent many summers trying to impress him. It never worked.

A favorite activity after swimming involved using the shower to clean off the salt and sand. We followed a curving hedge of fragrant cedars along a narrow wooden walkway leading to a dressing room located under the house. We left the brilliant sunshine and were temporally blinded as we entered a pitch black, expansive cellar. A string attached to a light fixture to illuminate our path remained elusive in the dark. We felt our way around, avoiding a misstep that might result in falling on to the dirt floor. Rena did not like dirty feet in the house, so we walked with care. The ice-cold water from the overhead shower evoked screams as it hit our warm skin. We felt around for our clothes that we had rolled up on the bench, hoping we walked out with our own outfits.

Later in the day everyone gathered at the fireplace on the side lawn overlooking the water as Al and the men readied things for a cookout and the women brought platters of corn on the cob, hot dogs, rolls, potato salad, and utensils from the kitchen. If the tide happened to be low, Al climbed down into the pump house to fetch wire buckets and clam rakes. The clam flats were a short walk down the beach. We gingerly tiptoed on the black slippery mud as it oozed between our toes. We stamped our feet in anticipation of a thin stream of water squirting into the air, signaling that clams (steamers), were underfoot.

Mary and I never retrieved more than a few. The thin-shelled, long-necked crustaceans were scrubbed and placed in a kettle filled with a few inches of water to steam. Within a few minutes we were all indulging in a feast of steamers dipped in warm, sweet butter.

The Townsend Girls, their spouses, children, and our family gathered at tables and chairs in the yard as the late afternoon sun set behind the diving raft and an evening chill began to fill the air. Tired, hungry, and happy, we readied ourselves for a feast.

I loved going to Touisset Point. Life didn't get any better.

Nellie

Nellie and her husband, Bill (McCloskey), lived about a five-minute walk from our house. After Bill died, Nellie came over a few nights a week to visit with my mother long after we had gone to bed. They relished talking politics and religion. Nellie never failed to pick up my current knitting project and knit as she and mom talked. The next morning, I had only to glance at my knitting.

"Mom, Nellie came over last night, didn't she?"

"Yes. How did you know?"

"Mom, her stitches are so tight compared to mine that I am going to have to rip them out."

"Oh, Nita, Nellie enjoys knitting. She's trying to help you along."

I guess I really didn't care because I was so fond of Nellie.

Nellie, like all the other Townsends, was fun and the most outspoken. She and Bill did not have children, so she enjoyed taking a keen interest in the three of us. Nellie freely gave her opinion on our clothes, what we were studying, or who we were dating. We liked the attention. She had an interest in and knowledge of all sorts of topics. She was fun to be around.

Nellie and my mother enjoyed walking. Neither of them drove, so if they wanted to have an adventure it involved using their feet to get there. Friends around town knew never to give them a ride.

"Don't pick up Ronnie and Nellie. They are out for their walk."

A favorite haunt of theirs involved going to the other side of town. They walked over the railroad tracks to the liquor store located in Riverside Square. Nellie and my mother enjoyed reading the labels on the bottles of wine and discussing what they knew about the region, be it France, Italy, or Spain. They were both interested in geography, especially my mother, who never ventured beyond the borders of the eastern United States. Following their "world tour" my mother occasionally purchased one bottle of vile-tasting Silver Satin wine. She would have a glass now and then, but mostly it remained in the cabinet under the kitchen sink gathering dust.

Even as a child I could tell that Nellie and Bill were very fond of each other. They carried on discussions, laughed together, and treated each other with kindness and affection. Bill remained good-natured and genial, considering the limitations rheumatoid arthritis put on his body. I never recall either one of them complaining.

Nellie, a student of comparative Bible study, attended classes at Providence College. She also belonged to the Daughters of Isabella, a Catholic organization which was the woman's auxiliary to the Knights of Columbus. She took this seriously. My mother did not. Once Nellie needed formal evening attire for an installation of officers. My mother pinned and basted one of Alicia's gowns that she had worn as a bridesmaid for Nellie to wear for the occasion. Mother worked on it, out of love for her friend, until Nellie looked as good as she could in a puffy, pink frock that was meant for someone decades younger. Nellie pinned her impressive Daughters of Isabella pin on her chest and went off to the meeting. I couldn't imagine what those ladies did in an organization with a name like that. I wondered if they sat around, ate fudge, and discussed Christopher Columbus.

Nellie lived the longest of all the Townsend Girls. She spent several years in the Riverside Nursing Home. I had the feeling she liked being there. When one of us happened to be in town we often stopped by to visit our friend. Invariably she would be on a sightseeing boat somewhere on Narragansett Bay enjoying a nursing home outing.

My sisters, Mary and Alicia, went to Nellie's wake when she died. They said that she looked lovely. Her face pale and powdered, her white hair in tight flat curls, and prominently displayed on Nellie's dress, her prized gold Daughters of Isabella pin.

Mary

Mary was called Tootie, but only by her sisters. She was married to Jimmy (Stockton), a man with boundless energy, and like his brothers-in-law, he was funny. They had one daughter, Joyce, and a black Scottie dog named Trubsie. The Stocktons lived just beyond Nellie and Bill in Chimney Corners, a development of attractive homes. Mary worked full time, unlike her sisters, who kept busy with volunteer work.

Mary's eyes sparkled when she looked at her husband, Jimmy. She, like everyone else, enjoyed listening to his latest joke.

Their daughter, Joyce, was pretty and smart. She attended a private girls' school and took piano lessons for many years. Being an only child lent itself, I thought, to these privileges.

When Alicia joined our family, Mary and I were ten and nine years old, Mary Stockton, one of the many people who came to visit, brought a gift to Alicia, but also something for her two older sisters. She reached into her pocketbook and presented each of us with a gift. We opened our pretty velvet-covered boxes, anticipating what treasure lay inside. We discovered a gold expansion bracelet adorned with an engraved heart, decorated with dainty pink flowers and tiny, pale green leaves. We slid them on our wrists and could not believe our good fortune: a new baby sister and an expansion bracelet.

Mary and Jimmy owned a summer cottage in Hope Valley, Rhode Island, a remote area northwest of Riverside and not far from the Connecticut line. Their cottage was rough and rustic, situated right on the lake and built, I believe, by Jimmy, my father, and some friends, one of whom had the incredible

Hope Valley summer house

name of Willy Wigglesworth. I discovered blueprints for a camp in my father's *Home Workshop Manual* that looked similar in design to the house in Hope Valley.

Going to Hope Valley always proved to be an adventure. We turned off onto a dirt road winding through hilly fields a mile or so before reaching the camp. Our journey was nearing an end when a wide, rusted metal gate blocked us from travelling any further. My father stopped the car and Mary and I ran to unhook the gate. Dad drove through and then we locked it and jumped back into the car. To us this signaled that our vacation was about to begin.

A screened-in porch ran across the front of the cabin, large enough to fit two folding cots, an assortment of dishes, food, and a stove. The rear two rooms I remember as having wall-to-wall cots. Each bed, covered in a scratchy brown warm Army blanket, kept the damp, cool nights at bay.

A short walk following a winding path through the woods dead-ended at a two-seater outhouse. Approaching the latrine you could smell the overpowering odor of a cleaning solution that Jimmy poured down on a regular basis. You always held your breath as well as your nose when making a brief visit to the outhouse. Rusty hinges caused the door to swing open, so you were always in fear of someone coming around the corner and seeing you sitting there. Worse than a human visitor was the possibility of encountering a snake. This area of Rhode Island was known for having snakes, big ones. We considered the outhouse a scary place. You did not dawdle.

As soon as Mary and I got out of our cots in the morning we ran outside to the cast-iron pump and poured some water down the shaft in order to prime it. The inner-workings of the pump squeaked and squealed as we jerked the handle several times up and down until water rolled off the lip. We collected the icy liquid in a metal pitcher and ran back to the porch so the adults could brew coffee. Jimmy held a match to the camp's propane stove, and nothing happened. On a second or third try a deafening, terrifying boom occurred, and a flame shot up almost to the ceiling of the porch, signaling that the old stove was lit. Everyone jumped back. One of the women made the coffee in a tall enamel pot and when ready poured the dark, aromatic brew into thick, white, heavy ceramic mugs. Eggs and bacon sizzled on the bent aluminum frying pans, and toast burned on the upright wire toaster. It smelled good and tasted even better.

Joyce gave us rides in the row boat and sometimes walked us to the outhouse. We were happy to have the protection of someone older and fearless. She helped us light firecrackers and sparklers on the fourth of July and joined her younger friends down at the lake for a swim.

The Stockton's boat

There were only a few cabins around the lake, but the one of interest, just beyond the hill, belonged to a Swedish family. Halfway down the slope leading to the water, a low, square structure, rumored to be a steam bath, demanded our attention. We heard that our neighbors were in the habit of sitting inside enjoying a hot, moist steam bath. They endured the heat until it became unbearable, thus forcing them to fling the door open, run down the hill and jump into the lake naked. We felt this to be valuable information and worth spending a fair amount of time looking in their direction for any activity. To our disappointment we failed to see anything, not even a member of the Swedish family out for a hike.

Joyce reading to Anita and Mary at Hope Valley

As children visiting Hope Valley, we needed to keep our guard up. There were snapping turtles in the lake as well as the possibility of snakes hiding in the rocks and underbrush. A nearby street had the unsettling name of Skunk Hill Road.

The tension of a possible encounter with unexpected wildlife added to the excitement and unending fun of camping at Hope Valley with our friends.

Florie

Florie and her husband, Fred (George), also lived in Riverside, and like Nellie and Bill, did not have children, which was probably a good thing, since Fred kept his wife very busy. They doted on their nieces and nephew, Joyce, Joan, and John. Florie had a special, endearing affection for John.

She liked to complain, but I don't think anyone paid too much attention to her. She often laughed quietly at something amusing, as if she did not want anyone to know she might be having a good time. Florie and Fred sent the exact same Christmas card, featuring two red and green bells, every year with their name printed inside as if they were business associates. Florie prayed a lot and remained a faithful volunteer at Meriam Hospital in Pawtucket for many years, but mostly she kept a close eye on Fred.

Fred was no dresser. I could not decide if he needed to gain weight to fit into his clothes or if he required a smaller size. He had large, bulbous eyes, a narrow face, prominent teeth, and a steel-grey mane of hair combed high on his head. Fred's plain looks were overshadowed by his outgoing, quirky personality.

Fred tried to amuse Florie with his antics, wise cracks, jokes, and long tales. Sometimes he succeeded. He worked for the same company, Proctor & Schwartz, as my dad, and Nellie's husband, Bill. Fred traveled frequently and on a business trip to Chicago he fell down a marble staircase and into the main lobby of the Biltmore Hotel injuring his head.

Florie's frequent reference to this incident never changed, "Why, Fred hasn't been the same since the accident."

We would roll our eyes at each other. Fred seemed no different after his fall than he did before the tumble: still the same old happy-go-lucky Fred.

One day we were all sitting around their yard chatting. The conversation turned to life and the hereafter. Florie announced that she wished she had died when she was five.

"If only God had allowed me to die when I was young, I would have gone straight to heaven and that would have been just fine with me," exclaimed Florie.

We all burst out laughing at her outlandish aspiration, but Florie stuck to her strange conviction.

When Fred retired, he found himself at a loss for things to do. He often arrived at our back door for a visit when our family was just ready to get into the car, or as my mother could be found kneeling with a brush and bucket scrubbing the kitchen floor. He was a master at appearing at the most inconvenient time. One day the doorbell rang. It was Fred. My mother got up from her sewing machine and invited him in. She took one look at the very slender, haphazardly dressed Fred, and exclaimed her usual,

"Glory be to Gawd, Fred, those pants need adjusting. Come in here and let me fix them."

Fred walked in, laughing.

"Fred, let me get a pair of Leo's trousers for you to put on while I fix yours."

My mother sewed a few wide tucks down the sides and waistline, then hiked up the trouser legs. She handed them back to Fred and he retreated to the bathroom to put on his proper fitting, shiny brown gabardine pants.

"They feel fine, Ronnie," he exclaimed, smiling, as he slipped his well-worn leather belt through the loops. "Thanks."

"Fred, every time I see you it looks as if your pants are going to slide to the ground. Bring what you have at home the next time you come by and I will take them all in for you."

My mother kept good to her promise and repaired Fred's wardrobe.

I sold lots of religious items to earn money for St. Brendan's School. Florie remained, year after year, an easy customer since most everything for sale had something to do with being a Catholic and she approved of that. I sold her a subscription to the diocesan newspaper each year, as well as crucifixes, small statues, and a plastic glow-in-the-dark rosary.

A few years following Fred's death, Florie entered the Riverside Nursing Home, just prior to her sister, Nellie, who would soon occupy an adjacent room. I stopped by to visit her on a trip back home. I entered her room. She lay flat on her back, eyes closed, hands folded on her chest, and wrapped around Florie's slender fingers, her plastic glow-in-the-dark rosary beads.

"I'm too late. She is dead," I thought.

I held my breath.

"Oh, my God, have I contributed to her death? I know those are the rosary beads I sold to her: the greenish glow, the iridescence. Could they have caused radiation poisoning? I am sure Florie has been praying on them for years."

I reached down and patted her hand. Her eyes suddenly opened. She glanced at me and the edges of her mouth turned up.

"Florie, it's me, Anita, Ronnie's daughter."

"Oh, Anita, Anita, I was just asking God to take me now and you came."

I could not help laughing.

We chatted for a while. In time, her eyes fluttered, and she dozed off. I paused in the doorway and glanced back at the all-too-familiar, suspect, glow-in-the-dark rosary beads.

God did not take Florie that afternoon per her prayerful request. She died in her sleep at the nursing home a few years later.

IN VOGUE

Not My Favorite Color

My mother liked me in brown. I never wear this color today. She sewed this brown scratchy wool snowsuit when I was four.

The hat, the jacket, and snow pants all matched, winning my approval.

Every time I received assistance putting this bulky ensemble on, I glanced at the felt umbrella my mother designed for the jacket. I wanted a snowflake, not a springtime umbrella.

Sometimes my mother did things I did not understand. This was the first, with more to come.

GETTING IN OVER MY HEAD

No Guts, No Glory

I stood on the far corner of the dock straining my eyes in the direction of the adults who were sitting in weathered Adirondack chairs on the hill overlooking the beach on Rena and Al's side lawn. I wasn't interested in them, but I was searching for that enigmatic, illusive, mysterious Jack Ratier. Mary and I had a fascination with Jack, always to no avail, but we kept trying to garner his attention.

Adults watching us swim from the yard

"Oh, he must be watching us from someplace," I thought to myself with a fair amount of unfounded confidence.

How could he not see me in my dazzling, new, two-piece buttercup yellow bathing suit that my mother had completed sewing only the day before? She had given it extra body by lining the entire outfit with some good quality cotton knit she just happened to have in her sewing room. Everyone had two-piece suits that summer, even my little four-year-old sister, Alicia.

I fluffed up the puffy pantaloons as I stood posing on the dock, contemplating my intended plunge. I backed up, stopped for a moment, then charged forward forcing myself out over the water as far as possible. I plummeted feet first hoping that Jack would see my dramatic entry from maybe his bedroom window partially hidden behind the hemlocks.

I experienced a profound chill as I descended with uncommon speed, into the dark recesses of the Kickamuit River. I frantically pointed my toes in an all-out effort to make contact with the soft, squashy river bottom. I quickly realized that a firmer platform was needed to propel me upward.

I floundered around but felt nothing. A slight sense of panic began to engulf me. My throat burned. I imagined I was somewhere short of the bottom. I balanced there in the darkness like a partially submerged bottle, not heavy enough to hit the bottom, yet not light enough to bob to the top.

I began to kick and claw at the water with the determination of a dog retrieving a bone buried under a mound of dirt. I struggled, hand-over-hand, as the sheer weight of my bathing suit impeded any progress. I had no air left when, to my surprise, my head popped up, breaking the water's surface. The white-washed dock was only a few feet away. I gulped a bite of lifesaving air and doggie paddled over to the ladder. My face felt hot and my breathing audible; only Alicia noticed.

I stood there as water poured out of my pantaloons: the fabric affixed to my skin like a suction cup stuck to a pane of glass.

What motivated my mother to line the entire bathing suit with absorbent cotton knit? Did she want to drown her middle daughter?

I reached up and ran my hand along the top of my bathing cap. By the sheer force of my entry it stood up on my head, pointed, like a silly gnome's hat.

I glanced over at Florence, our next-door neighbor, who my mother had invited to

*Alicia looks back at me
standing on the dock
following my ascent*

join us at the beach. She was sitting on a low bench with Alicia. Florence had donned her bathing cap while I was submerged. There perched on her head, looking much like a giant mushroom, sat a plastic kitchen bowl cover.

What an embarrassment! Did Mrs. Overdeep just open the refrigerator and snatch it off a bowl covering some leftover lettuce?

I wanted to die, to vanish right there on the spot, without so much as a ripple. I took a quick side glance at the front lawn. I could still see only Rena and my mother: no Jack. I breathed a sigh of relief.

Florence with her salad-cover bathing cap and Alicia

Mary, Florence, and I continued to jump off the diving board and the side of the dock. I no longer took a running start. My father, who had been watching us and taking pictures, announced it was time to go. We gathered our towels and walked to the basement shower room to change.

Rena, always the gracious hostess, invited us for supper. I knew my mother's reply even before she uttered her response. We had brought along a guest and dinner, no matter how informal, went beyond her ability to accept. I was glad since I did not want Jack to sit across the table from us and possibly say anything about what he may have seen out at the dock. I should not have worried since he would have done his usual: say nothing and ignore us.

We hopped in the car for the drive home. I rolled down the back window yelling a big thank you to Rena and Al as they waved from the driveway. My father shifted the car into low gear and we climbed the hill in the direction of Warren and on to Riverside.

I glanced out the rear window just as we were about to turn the corner. Jack was nowhere to be seen.

SMOKE SCREEN

I Owe You

"Don't you dare let go. My feet haven't touched the shingles yet."

My sister, Mary, held my wrists tight as I directed her on what to do in an all-too-loud stage whisper. I could feel the edge of the windowsill cut into my ribs as I lay on my stomach struggling to back out of our second-floor bedroom window. I stretched my body attempting to make contact with the tip of my shoe on the pitched roof. No luck. Finally, my shoe hit the roof with a deafening thud. I froze.

"Don't worry, no one is below in the breakfast room now," Mary reassured me.

I wanted to agree with her, but I could only concentrate on my immediate pain. This aerobic act was a dangerous venture during the daytime, but in the dark of a moonless night it was akin to descending into the abyss of a storm drain.

The wind caught my skirt. It billowed out like the bloated belly of a whale. I yanked one of my hands free of Mary's grasp and attempted to tuck the errant plaid pleated skirt under my knees.

"I hope the neighbors didn't see that," I mumbled.

"Quit worrying. It's too dark," Mary exclaimed. "No one is out there at night, unless it's Mr. Lemos in his garden checking his string beans with a flashlight. I don't see anything going on. Relax."

Downstairs the front doorbell rang. We could hear familiar loud greetings and laughter. My parents' best friends were arriving for an evening of canasta. They could be counted on to make a lot of noise. I heard Jimmy Stockton's infectious laugh. Mary and I exchanged glances and we laughed too. We heard Jimmy's wife, Mary, chime in with her high-pitched, cheery voice.

Things were quiet for a moment, then my mother's good friend, Nellie, said something and there was laughter again. We felt safe knowing their downstairs commotion would drown out any noise we were making.

The soles of both my shoes were now firmly on the roof. My elbows gripped the window sill and I ached from trying to keep my head arched for better balance.

Mary walked over to her bed and reached under her pillow. She produced an open pack of L&M cigarettes and a book of matches. She dragged a match across the abrasive strip and it ignited on the first try. She put the cigarette end between her lips, lit the tip, and inhaled with adult-like finesse. A bright red glow appeared on the end. Mary walked over and handed me the cigarette. I inhaled. We both began to laugh, bringing on a fit of coughing for me. Mary never choked or coughed. She knew when to talk, when to inhale, and the right moment to exhale. Each time I smoked it seemed as if I was experiencing it for the first time. I was just not as proficient and skilled at it as my sister, but this never stopped me from trying to improve my technique.

Mary lit her cigarette and took a lengthy inhale, then handed her cigarette for me to hold while she proceeded to back out the window: agile, graceful, and sure of herself.

Not long into our forbidden activity, we both heard the door open at the bottom of the stairs.

"Is someone smoking up there?"

My mother did not wait for an answer.

"The two of you come to the top of the stairs, now."

Mary and I scrambled head first through the open window, landing on the floor with the cigarettes held high. We quickly snuffed them out in Mary's tiny portable silent butler. Her handy little gadget was the size of fifty cent piece with a handle and a hinged lid. The device was easy for her to conceal just about anywhere.

We ran around the bedroom waving our arms frantically attempting to disperse the smoke.

I opened the bedroom door and we stepped out on to the landing at the top of the stairs facing my mother below.

We said nothing.

"Were you two smoking?"

Mary's response was as if she had practiced it beforehand.

"No, Mom, it was only me. Nita wasn't smoking."

I could not believe what I was hearing. I would have liked Mary to repeat her reply, but I knew better.

"Get to bed, the two of you."

The downstairs door closed.

We didn't say a word to each other, but put on our night clothes, turned out the light, and climbed into our beds. I could hear Mary take a deep breath.

"Mary, you covered up for me."

"That's okay. Mom knows I sneak smoking all the time, but she thinks you are as pure as the driven snow."

I didn't want Mary to know that I agreed with her assessment, so I let out a little grunting sound as acknowledgement that I heard what she said.

My mother told me more than once, "You were such a little devil of sorts when you were young, always getting into trouble, but once you turned thirteen things changed. You were easy."

I couldn't relax. I pulled the cover up tight over my shoulders, turning and tossing trying to get comfortable. The taste of tobacco lingered in my mouth. I ran my tongue over my teeth. I cleared my throat, swishing saliva around in my mouth. I coughed then cleared my throat again.

"Will you stop that infernal noise over there? I can't get to sleep."

"Sorry, Mar, I'll be quiet. Night. Thanks for not squealing on me to mom."

"Yeah. Sure."

ACTS OF LOVE

Dad's Best Friend

The last rays of late afternoon sun streamed through the small cellar window. This hazy band of light shed an eerie glow on the artificial hand that lay atop my father's workbench. I picked up the rigid form in my twelve-year-old hands and examined the piece, turning it over and over.

Rheumatoid arthritis was rapidly claiming the once robust body of my father's best friend and former co-worker, Bill McClusky. The inflexible hand represented just one of the many things my dad designed to make Bill's life more bearable. Bill, a big strapping guy, with thinning hair, and a smile that never quit, appeared fit enough to play guard for the Providence College Friars basketball team, but his days were spent in a wheelchair situated next to a side window in his living room. He looked out at homes very much like the neat Cape Cod house he shared with his beloved, faithful, and frequently funny wife, Nellie.

His legs and torso were becoming increasingly inflexible. His right-hand fingers began to curl inward. My father thought a form to fit Bill's hand would help alleviate some of the curvature. He took the necessary measurements and designed and constructed a stainless-steel hand for Bill. A flat piece of metal with five circular straight tubes was fashioned to fit his fingers and thumb. This enabled them to lay straight. A strap secured the entire device to his right hand.

The little invention worked for a while, but in time it became evident that it was not going to forestall any crippling effect. This did not deter my father. He went on to construct a stationary exercise bike. He also fashioned and installed a Hoyer Lift that assisted Nellie in lowering and raising Bill into the tub. It was a large contraption and, when not in use, the bulky swing occupied the main hall just outside the bathroom. I used to examine the lift, trying to figure out how the pulleys and chains worked. It looked complicated to me, but the premise was just a simple machine.

Mary, Alicia, and I loved to visit our friend.

"I'm on my way to see Bill. Anyone want to come?" called dad.

We never needed to be asked twice.

"Wait for me. Wait for me!" we yelled as we came running, ready to climb into the car for the short ride to Charlotte Street.

Bill was just one of those happy people. When we entered the living room, he greeted us with the same line every time.

"How about a chicken bone?"

We laughed each time he said it and then helped ourselves to the long, thin candies with chocolate centers that always sat in a glass jar on the window ledge.

Then Bill looked at my father and chimed in with his second predictable question,

"Leo, how did an old frog like you get three such beautiful daughters?"

On one of those visits we heard that Bill had volunteered to take two experimental drugs for research being done at the Peter Bent Brigham Hospital in Boston. None of us knew at the time how important these trials would be for people in the future. He was one of the first patients to volunteer to receive cortisone and be injected with gold.

I do not know if Bill received any relief from these unproven drugs, but I remember his physical appearance began to change. His hands and legs swelled as did his face. Bill's cheeks were round and rosy, and his eyes seemed to sink deeper into his swollen face. Even with these visible setbacks he continued to remain hopeful that cortisone and gold would successfully slow the progression of the disease.

On warm days Nellie rolled Bill in his wheelchair out on the ramp my father had constructed on their sunny side porch. I liked to ride my bike over, hoping to find Bill outside. He wanted to know what I was up to and always seemed to have a funny tale about one of the notorious O'Rourke kids who lived around the corner. On summer-like days an O'Rourke could be counted on to skip school. Bill entertained himself watching the white police car cruising up and down the neighborhood streets looking for the truant. Bill all the while just sat there smiling, knowing the exact location of the O'Rourke hiding place.

My father never faltered in his love and concern for his best friend. Bill's valiant struggle to stay alive ended at home, with Nellie by his side, on his birthday, August 28, 1950.

Nellie waked him at home in the living room next to the window where he spent so many years of his life. I rode my bike over to their home on Charlotte Street to say goodbye for the final time. I climbed the porch steps and knocked on the screen door. Our dear family friend, Joan, Bill's college-age niece, invited me in. I stepped into the kitchen and glanced ahead. I could see Bill through the hall entryway laying in his casket with his head on a pillow, as if he had just laid down for an afternoon nap. I stopped and could go no further. I began to cry. Joan put her arm around me and led me out to the porch. She drew me in close to her and consoled me as I sobbed.

"It is not necessary that you go in to see Bill. He knows you are here."

Joan embraced me as I leaned against her. I tried to say thank you, but the words would not come. She gave me another reassuring hug. I turned, ran over to my bike, and peddled home.

IN VOGUE

Almost Twins

Nancy Connor and I were best friends from ninth grade through the twelfth grade.

We loved to take the bus into Providence every now and then to clothes shop on a Saturday.

On one such adventure, we each purchased nearly identical white Ship'n Shore blouses. Mine featured red buttons and red decorative stitching. Nancy's was trimmed in blue.

I wore my blouse with a blue wrap-around chambray cotton skirt. The chances of it flying open were good as I climbed the hill that ran parallel to Narragansett Bay on my long trek to Riverside Junior High.

Nancy and I liked to wear our almost matching blouses on the same day. We thought we looked pretty neat.

GOOD FOLKS

A Pleasure to Know you

I heard it coming before I saw it.

"Yoo-hoo, yoo-hoo, Mary, Anita hop in. I'll drop you off at the end of Harris Street."

Mrs. Haskins, my Brownie leader, always offered us a ride in bad weather. We were running home for lunch from St. Brendan's School in the pouring rain. The car came to a gliding stop and I glanced over into the back seat of the dull, grey, old-fashioned automobile. The car was what we referred to as a rattletrap.

Haskins kids were everywhere, all squeezed in next to each other. Bowbee, the oldest, held Little Emma. Little Arthur, having been pushed so far into the corner, was almost out of sight. Winkie sat next to him holding Baby James. The front seat, empty except for the driver, Mrs. Haskins, Big Emma, provided the only place left for us to sit. The *big* and *little* prefixes were how some of the Haskins children were addressed, except for Bowbee, Baby James, and Winkie.

Mary and I, dripping wet, shouted thanks for the ride and hustled into the front seat out of the rain. I gave the door a mighty slam. Mrs. Haskins shifted into first gear and the car lurched forward. The right front tire hit a sizable pothole. A jet of cold, dirty water splashed up through a gaping hole in the floor and on to my legs like a shot from a giant water pistol. I made a face, and shifted my position. Mary looked at me and smiled with a knowing grin. She had gotten the middle seat, the good seat. I sat next to the door attempting to avoid the yawning hole in the floor, but I had failed. I braced myself for another cold splash, but Mrs. Haskins must have noticed me thrust my legs into the air and avoided any further depressions.

159

The Haskins family of seven lived about a half mile from us in a Cape Cod house they built, but never quite finished. It had that uncompleted look, and it was difficult to tell what exactly needed to be done. They lived with Grandma Durgan. She came to Riverside from Ireland to be with her daughter's family. She helped with just about everything around the house and took over completely when Mrs. Haskins was called to substitute teach.

Mr. Haskins, Big Arthur, worked at WJAR, a major radio station, in Providence. He did technical things that helped produce the shows on the air, but when television promised to be the wave of the future, he went back to school and learned how to become a cameraman.

Thinking they would not be able to have a family, they adopted Bowbee (Roberta), but they were wrong. Winkie (Kathleen) came along and soon after, their first boy, Little Arthur, joined the growing family. Another daughter, Little Emma, followed. A few years went by and Baby James was born.

Mr. and Mrs. Haskins were both scout leaders. Mr. Haskins' Boy Scout uniform looked just right on his trim body. Mrs. Haskins' green Girl Scout leader's dress and hat were as official but appeared a bit unkempt. Her salt-and-pepper hair, curled from an occasional home permanent, was never a neat fit under her Scottish style uniform hat. Her large bosom, and soft, somewhat lumpy figure, made her look exactly what she was, a very busy and involved mom of five young children.

They were different from us, but in some ways, similar. We went to the same school and church. My mother and Mrs. Haskins were both

My Brownie membership card from 1946

Girl Scout leaders and good friends, but not best friends like the four Townsend sisters. Mr. and Mrs. Haskins and their family were fun to be around.

Things were casual at 39 Woodbine Street. Once I knocked on the back door and Grandma Durgan called for me to come in. The door wouldn't budge. I peeked though the pane of glass and saw a huge mound of laundry piled high against the door waiting for a trip to the basement to be washed. I pushed with all my might and yelled. In time someone came, gave the laundry a kick, and opened the door.

Mr. Haskins, as far as Mary and I were concerned, had a dream job. He worked at our favorite radio station. Occasionally on a Saturday, he would take Bowbee, Winkie, Mary, and me to WJAR. This was about as close as we could get from Riverside, Rhode Island, to Hollywood, California. He allowed us to sit in a small room alongside a window that overlooked an area below where the actual broadcasting was taking place. We were warned to be quiet since our voices would carry down to the sound stage, thus interfering with the live show.

Cecelia Monroe, a local piano instructor, hosted a children's talent show each Saturday morning. A nervous child sat alone at a grand piano and played under the attentive gaze of Miss Monroe. The tap dancers watched from the front row awaiting their turn.

The dancers provided us with real entertainment. They did their routine in black shoes polished to a blinding shine. The boys were all neatly dressed in dark pants and white, long-sleeve shirts and the girls outfitted in fancy dresses. No one saw them exhibit their talent except their families sitting in the audience, the radio staff, and the four kids looking down from the observation window. The microphone hung low catching every nuance of the metal taps clickity-clacking on the linoleum floor. We all knew that it was peculiar to be tap dancing over the radio but kept this fact to ourselves. Being a guest at the station was such a privilege that we never considered jeopardizing our presence with talking and giggling.

On another visit to the radio station I recall leaning forward to get a better look at the action below. My two long braids were in the way of my viewing so I gave them a quick flick back. At this very moment, Art Lake, THE star broadcaster at WJAR walked behind where I sat. He gave my long pigtails a gentle tug. I turned, and he smiled at me and welcomed us all to the radio station. I knew then, at that moment, I had almost met the equivalent of a movie star.

In addition to working long hours at the radio station, Mr. Haskins instructed Little Arthur and other boys in scouting as well as sewing for his family. As spring approached the only thing any girl desired was to walk down the aisle at the children's 9 a.m. Mass at St. Brendan's Church on Easter morning wearing a new spring coat and hat. Mr. Haskins somehow knew this.

I knocked on their door one afternoon hoping to find a playmate. Mr. Haskins yelled for me to come in. "I'm in the living room. Come see what I am doing."

Fabric was everywhere. He was sitting at an old, black sewing machine near the fireplace. He smiled and laughed as he told me about his project.

"I am sewing Young Emma, Winkie, and Bowbee coats and matching hats for Easter.

"I like the color, Mr. Haskins."

I gazed in amazement at the mounds of creamy, green wool flannel draped on the sofa, over chairs, but mostly in piles on the floor.

"They will all be dressed alike. It's not Kelly green, but a slightly different shade of green. What do you think?"

"I really like it, Mr. Haskins. I didn't know you could sew." He just laughed and kept on going with his project.

"They are so lucky." I thought, "Bowbee, Winkie and Little Emma will all be dressed alike for Easter."

Matching clothes, in those days, constituted the ultimate fashion statement. Mary and I did have some identical outfits sewn by my mother from the same Simplicity pattern, but I am sure it represented an economy measure more than anything else. Using the same sewing guide meant she did not have to purchase two. Mother made us identical sunsuits, but not quite. The outfits were alike except for the rickrack edging sewn on in contrasting colors: Mary's white and mine red. Separate, but equal, seemed to be the way my mother did things.

My father, like Mr. Haskins, could sew and used my mother's sewing machine to make striped,

Mary and me posing with Dad
in our matching sunsuits, 1944

canvas awnings for our house one very hot summer. He wanted to shield the kitchen, the dining, and living rooms from the west sun, but for aesthetic reasons he made them for the entire house. My dad told me he learned tailoring when he was a young boy in the orphanage and could sew buttonholes on garments. I wondered if he knew how to make three girls identical spring coats: big ones for Mary and me and a cute toddler size for my little sister, Alicia. Well, Mr. Haskins knew how to do this, and I couldn't wait to see his girls on Easter morning all dressed in matching outfits.

In time, Girl Scouting and our connection with the Haskins family faded as we grew older. I did carry on the tradition as a Cub Scout leader for four years. I learned quickly that energy was a major component in leading a troop of exuberant young boys.

I don't recall hearing about Mr. Haskins dying, but my sister, Alicia, happened to be in Rhode Island one day and heard that Mrs. Haskins was being cared for at her home in the final stages of cancer.

Alicia drove over to Woodbine Street and knocked on the door. Roberta (Bowbee) welcomed her in. She led her into Mrs. Haskins' bedroom. Alicia glanced at our former scout leader lying there: thin, sunken cheeks, motionless, and with her eyes shut.

Alicia told me, "She did not resemble in any way the energetic, spirited woman with the infectious laugh of years past. I sat down next to her and leaned forward telling her who I was, but I wondered if she could hear me. I looked at the fresh bed linens. They were smooth and flat as if they had been gently patted down over her thin frame in a loving gesture by her daughter. I did not sense a feeling of sadness in the room as Roberta tended to her mother. I will never forget the tranquility and deep peace I felt. It seemed to envelop every corner of the room."

These two partners in life, Big Arthur and Big Emma, did not reach old age, but their job was done. They were an example to all those they encountered of how to conduct oneself in life: with kindness, service, fun, and a sense of purpose. They were good folks.

Neighbors

Neighborhood

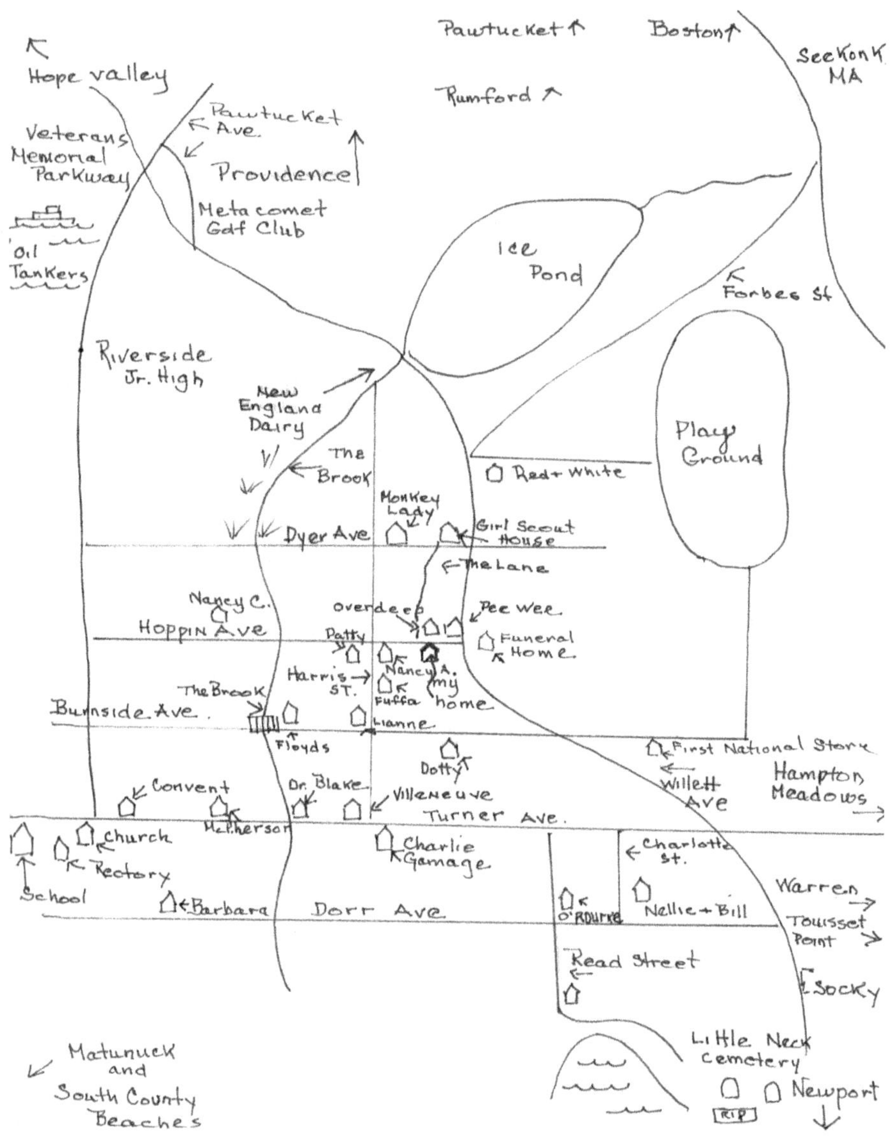

THE OVERDEEP FAMILY

Fine Neighbors

Mother always said they were just too short. Her comment was not intended as criticism toward our neighbor's stature. She was referring to the Scottish shortbread cookies frequently baked by Mrs. Overdeep in their warm, sweet-smelling kitchen. The pale, round, dense cookies filled with butter, cream, eggs, and sugar were a child's delight, but too rich for my mother's plain taste.

The Overdeep family of three (Georgina, Gerald, and their daughter, Florence,) lived across the street from us for all the years I lived in Riverside. Their brown-stained home featured a very steep sloped roof that looked different from the bungalow and Victorian houses in our neighborhood. A tall privet hedge surrounded their entire property. Mr. Overdeep took great pride in its orderly appearance,

The Overdeep family home

giving the hedge regular trims with his long hand-held trimmers. These neighbors were an important part of my growing-up years.

Mrs. Overdeep came to the United States as a young woman from England, securing a job in Providence as a cook for Professor Couch, an ancient history professor at Brown University.

She often called you not by your given name, but *my dear.* Mrs. Overdeep embodied the term old-fashioned. She had a long thin nose, a pretty square jaw line, beautiful sky-blue eyes, sandy colored hair, and a diminutive, but well-proportioned figure. Her high-pitched voice, often uneven in tone, made you pay close attention to what she was saying.

Mrs. Overdeep's plain cotton housedress, always protected by an apron tied in the back with a perfect bow, made up her daily attire, except for Sundays when she attended Riverside Congregational Church and wore, like us, her dressy clothes. For trips to the trash barrel located near the garage, she wrapped a hand-crocheted shawl around her slim shoulders. Mrs. Overdeep had two or three shawls that she made in dull colors of tan or brown, trimmed with fringe. To me they seemed efficient and less work than buttoning up a sweater, but I wondered if she shivered as the damp, cold wind invaded all the open spaces in the crocheted design during the wintertime. She hung these handmade wraps, ready and waiting, on hooks in the back hall.

I do not remember Mrs. Overdeep as ever being idle. She crocheted intricate patterns of grapes and leaves into doilies while carrying on a conversation the entire time. She gave me one of her lovely creations when I became engaged to be married. She knit countless mittens and hats to keep poor children warm in foreign lands and cooked lots of sweets, as well as three meals a day for her small family.

Mr. Overdeep, called Gerald, was a tall man with a deep voice, thinning hair, pale eyes, a fair complexion, and very big feet, larger than any man I knew. He affectionally referred to his wife as Juttie and not Georgina. He came to the United States as a young man from the Netherlands. He told us stories of his life as a young boy skating to school on the frozen canals during the cold winter months. I imagined him with tweed, woolen britches and an oversized blouse featuring full, wide long sleeves. A hand-knit watch cap pulled down

(Mrs O_)

Just imagine a little "Cheekee"
Of about 5 feet and two,
That describes my dear intended
"She is mrs O' to you"—
So when you ever meet her
She with her hat askew,
You'll say she is an angel
"But she's mrs O. to you"
Her hair is golden yellow
Her eyes a deep sea blue,
You'll like and adore her
"Still she's mrs O. to you"
Then when you taste her cooking
Especially her stew,
Just keep on remembering
"She's mrs O. to you"
And when you come to know her
And love her as I do,
Do not forget one moment
"She's mrs O. to you"—

Mr. Overdeep composed this poem for his "Juttie"

over his ears kept his head warm as he took long-legged strides on his wooden-blade ice skates. I could see him leaning into the wind, hands clasped behind his back, gliding down the Zider Zee. It was nice to have neighbors who came from the faraway lands featured in my boxed book set of *Children Around the World.*

Mr. Overdeep retired early from the Standard Oil Company and seemed to do fix-it jobs around the house for the remainder of his life. He wore boots and sturdy work clothes outside but, once in the house, he slipped on his brown, leather slippers with elastic inserts on the sides. He wore a Perry Como style sweater with buttons down the front. It was grey and looked very itchy.

I thought Florence, their one child, resembled the little girl on the cover of the "Old Dutch Cleanser" can. Tall, thin, with straight, blond hair cut in the style of a "Dutch Cut," she was pretty in a delicate way. Mr. Overdeep told me they picked her name so she would not have a nickname. I thought this odd because he called his wife Juttie, not Georgina.

Florence often played in her yard behind the dense privet hedge. Mr. Overdeep constructed a gate at the back entrance so Florence could not get out. I believed this captivity to be just one of the unspoken rules of being an only child. There were three of us and we were free to see the world from our fenceless yard. The plight of the only child remained a mystery to me, but I respected the strange rules and felt the protection of the single offspring to be of grave importance.

A large iron floor register, located in the hall between their living room and kitchen, provided Mary, Florence, and me with occassional entertainment during the winter months. We would stand on top of the grating for long periods of time in anticipation of the furnace turning on. With the sudden blast of hot air, we laughed and twirled like three whirling dervishes in dizzying circles as our skirts bellowed out.

Down in their basement, near the enormous wicker steamer trunk that Mrs. Overdeep packed her belongings in for the trip to the states, rows of long-necked, brown, glass bottles were neatly lined up on a

Mary, Florence, and me sitting in their side yard

shelf ready to be filled with homemade root beer. We were banned from the cellar once Mrs. Overdeep capped the bottles. The root beer needed time to age. On occasion, a bottle would explode with a deafening boom. This unexpected detonation never failed to startle the upstairs occupants.

In one corner of their yard they planted a small vegetable garden. Tall, deep-green, leafy swiss chard grew alongside strange-looking very small cabbage-like plants that I learned were Brussels sprouts. My mother was the recipient of surplus tomatoes and lettuce, but Mrs. Overdeep knew better than to give us anything as English as Swiss chard or Brussels sprouts.

During the summertime at three p.m. sharp I would often find myself knocking at the Overdeep's back door. Everything stopped for tea at three in their household. Her warm greeting, "Come in, my dear," never changed. Mrs. Overdeep ushered me into the kitchen, making room for me around the table. Mr. Overdeep sat on a large, dark stained wooden chair with a tall back and arm rests. To his left a small table held a blue metal can of Prince Albert tobacco, a box of matches, a cardboard container holding white, paper-thin cigarette tissues, a book or two, and a Bible.

Making tea took an insurmountable amount of time. The pot of water on the gas stove signaled it was ready when a shrill whistle pierced the air. To keep the teapot from cracking, Mrs. Overdeep swished hot water around the inside. After a minute or two she discarded the water and measured loose tea into the pot before adding the boiling water from the stove. She encased the pot in a tea cozy and we waited.

Large white cups fetched from the kitchen cabinet were passed around and the tin of sweets, usually raisin-filled tarts or buttery shortbread cookies the size of silver dollars, appeared out of nowhere. My mouth salivated as I tried to settle on my choice. Sometimes we were offered seconds.

Mrs. Overdeep poured the steaming tea into my cup and did not stop until the hot liquid reached the brim. I could only cool it off with the smallest bit of milk. This did not make me happy, but I knew my gracious hostess was on to my game. I came for the sweets, a fast cup of lukewarm tea, and then a quick dash out the back door. The fact that Mrs. Overdeep saw through my thin veneer of greed didn't bother me. I came back for teatime again and again.

When Mr. Overdeep finished his afternoon tea he pushed his cup to the center of the table and reached over to retrieve a sheet of cigarette tissue and his can of tobacco. He laid the paper on the table and placed several long chunks of tobacco on top. He rolled the paper around the tobacco, picked it up, and ran his tongue along the thin line of glue to seal the cigarette, then he scraped the match along the strip of sandpaper on the side of the match box and ignited the tip of his newly crafted cigarette. With a puff or two the tip invariably burst into flames. He'd blow it out, laugh, and begin again. When it was lit to his satisfaction, Mr. Overdeep closed his eyes, leaned back in his chair, and inhaled with a deep, slow breath.

We spent hours during summer vacation enjoying the comfort of the wicker chairs on their long front porch hidden behind tall arborvitaes and the privet fence. Mrs. Overdeep taught Mary and me to crochet and embroider, exhibiting endless patience at our many attempts to attain the correct results. I hope we remembered to tell Mrs. Overdeep that the crochet-decorated shampoo towel Mary made for my mother was a favorite gift. We all used it until it became threadbare.

Florence, four years younger than me, and I played with each other when our own friends were not around. I liked to be invited to her playroom on the second floor. The

Mrs. and Mr. Overdeep

room contained dolls of all sorts, carriages to wheel them in, cradles to rock them, and toys of every sort. I mostly sat on the floor and looked around the tidy playroom and admired its contents.

Sometimes during our vacation from school in the summer, we delivered invitations to everyone in the neighborhood to one of the plays that we put on in the Overdeep's garage. Surprisingly, people would come. A bed sheet hung almost across the width of the garage on a wire and separated the card table chairs awaiting an audience from the backstage area. The strong smell of gasoline permeated Florence's garage. Mrs. Overdeep cleaned her husband's felt hats in a vat of gasoline that sat on a table against the back wall. She thought it did a nice job and was economical. My mother never relaxed when we were in that one-car garage. She fully expected the entire structure to jettison skyward, but her fears never came to fruition.

During the summertime on warm Sunday afternoons, Mr. Overdeep often invited me to join his family for a ride. Florence and I squeezed ourselves into the back of his two-door Ford coupe. He said he did not think having a four-door car was necessary when two doors did the job. Cars, he told me, need not be comfortable since it was necessary that the driver remain alert. The discomfort of their car extended into the rear seat. Florence and I anxiously waited for the ride to commence as we wiggled, attempting to get comfortable on the warm prickly wool upholstered seats. The destination remained the same on most trips: leaving Rhode Island and going just over the state line to Seekonk, Massachusetts, to buy vanilla ice cream cones. We always hoped our short trip would be to our favorite ice cream stand that was constructed in the shape of a giant wooden milk bottle. After enjoying our treat, Mr. Overdeep turned the car around and we began our two-mile journey back to Riverside.

On the days Florence's mother baked she often made an extra braided sweet roll for us. The nut-and-fruit-filled confection topped with buttercream frosting did not last long at our house. On my mother's 50th birthday our thoughtful neighbor baked her an English birthday cake. I overheard Mrs. Overdeep whisper to my mother that she soaked the raisin filling in rum overnight.

On the day my father died, I looked out the front window and watched as Mrs. Overdeep walked across the street, grasping her hand-crocheted shawl around her slim body against the October chill. She held a plate containing her wonderful, sweet, braided bread. It never tasted better than it did on that day.

Neither the tall, stately, hedge nor the dark brown stain on the clapboards of their home ever changed. They remained a quiet household without a cross word or a shout. Our good neighbors, the Overdeeps, were considerate, kind people who helped weave a pattern of sameness and comfort into our lives.

I have only to close my eyes and I can still hear, "Come in, my dear," as Mrs. Overdeep welcomed me in for tea at three.

SANDWICHED

New Kid on the Block

For the first nine years of my life I delighted in being the baby in our small family. My sister, Mary, was eighteen months my senior. I was often referred to simply as *The Baby* and not Anita. I found great comfort in that protective title. It wrapped around me like a cozy security blanket. Everything changed one warm June day, Friday the 13th to be exact, when my little sister came into the world.

My mother, a wise woman, gave Mary and me the responsible but happy task of naming this newest and final addition to our family. She was christened Alicia Catherine: Alicia, the name of a favorite nun at our school, and Catherine, a common name on the maternal side of our family.

Alicia's Christening,
Aunt Alice holding her
niece, 1947

My repositioning in the family structure was immediate. I became forever the middle child. Mary's spot never changed. My future looked bumpy as the rough holes left behind in the wake of an early summer gully washer. The mountains to climb appeared shrouded under a blanket of mist and mystery, defying the most skilled of climbers. Life looked uncertain for me. The new baby loomed larger than her seven pounds eight ounces.

Ignoring her did not seem to work. Her big brown eyes, sweet smile, and rosy, pink skin invited you to hang out in her company. Alicia was a good baby and cried very little. She had the unique

175

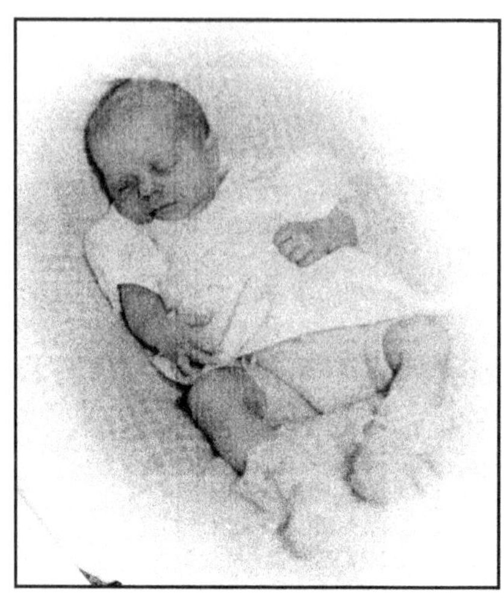

*Alicia, a good baby,
enjoyed her naps*

honor of being the only baby in the entire neighborhood.

When Alicia was a few months old, my mother allowed our playmates to come over to take turns holding the baby. Peggy Marquette, a teenager my mother considered to be very responsible, organized the event. The neighbor kids lined up on our front porch and down the steps. Peggy sat on the wooden swing attached to sturdy chains secured into the ceiling, while holding baby Alicia. Everyone had to wait their turn. Peggy passed the baby on to each of the motley group of neighborhood boys and girls. She then gave the swing a gentle push. Mary and I found ourselves standing in line like everyone else. We were just part of the crowd and dutifully waited Peggy's direction to hold our baby sister.

Mary and I often pushed Alicia in the old wicker carriage along the sidewalk on Harris Street and down the rough, unpaved lane up to the Girl Scout house. Sometimes the back wheel of the carriage careened off its moorings and flew out into the street. One of us would retrieve it, click it back on, and we would continue on with our journey. We played with her, fed her, and sometimes ignored her and went on our way with friends.

As *The Baby* grew older we read her stories. I soon discovered that reading James Whitcomb Riley's *Little Orphan Annie* scared Alicia. I would inflect my voice while reading key lines...

*and **shooooo** the chickens off the porch
and earn her board and keep...
and all us children when supper things is done
would sit around the kitchen fire and have the
mostest fun a-listening to the witch tales...*

*Mary and me posing with Alicia and the
unpopular baby carriage*

Alicia, at this point, yelled to my mother, "Mommy, Anita is scaring me again."

My mother hastened into the living room at a fast pace to rescue Alicia. I received my usual stern reprimand.

I learned early on that having attention directed on the oldest and the youngest proved advantageous. Mary, the Lewis and Clark of our trio, blazed the trail for me. Alicia took on the title of the baby and, even today, continues to be forever young.

This focus on the first and the last child afforded me autonomy and freedom to glide merrily along, frequently unnoticed. I slipped through those years taking advantage of and loving my new and unexpected role within the family unit.

As adults, my sister Alicia sent me this birthday card
as a reminder that she has not forgotten

IN VOGUE

A Gift Gone Awry

Just too fancy for me

One Christmas I received a semi-see-through blouse studded with rhinestones. It was so far out of my comfort zone that I searched for words attempting to say thank you for a piece of clothing I disliked even before I had it fully out of the box.

I hated the glitzy fake diamond decoration scattered over the blouse front. I did not like cap sleeves. They were uncomfortable and not as finished looking as set-in sleeves. The almost see-through top meant someone could possibility view my slip and bra straps.

I did decide to wear it to a New Year's Eve party that I had been invited to in high school.

I needed something stunning to distract from the elaborate blouse. I embarked on a mission to sew an aqua taffeta full circle skirt. The day of the party I decided to blind-stitch the entire circular hem, a formidable self-inflicted torture. I completed the hem minutes prior to my date's arrival.

I ran upstairs, dressed, and scurried back down in full regalia to answer the front door.

My date looked at me and exclaimed: *Oh, it's real informal. No one is dressing up.* I wanted to cry, but I didn't. I know my mother could have cried right along with me.

A PERFECT BITE

Teething

Proper care and maintenance of your teeth required visits to Dr. Moore. Your turn in the dentist's chair came soon after the appearance of a set of permanent teeth.

My mother made a dentist appointment for herself only if a dental emergency occurred. Her teeth, big with ample space between the front incisors, were a nice addition to her pretty smile. My sister, Mary, and I were not so lucky to pick and choose when we had a rendezvous with the dentist.

A visit to Dr. Moore meant a trip into Providence on the red New England Transportation Company bus. Lunch followed an appointment, complete with dessert, at the Boston Store cafeteria and, if time allowed, shopping at one or two of the major department stores in Providence. The post-dental enticements were enough to make me forget about the excruciatingly painful grinding of the drill into a tooth or, even more frightening, the close proximity of Dr. Moore's thick, black, prickly appearing mustache that came dangerously close to touching my right cheek.

The formidable grey five-story Howard Building housed Dr. Moore's office on the fifth and highest floor. The elevator that transported you to your destination resembled a barred monkey cage you might encounter at the zoo. The swaying cables supporting and suspending the elevator were visible from all sides. Your trip up began with just the simple act of waiting for the elevator to descend. You had several minutes to examine the cables doing their horizontal and vertical jig in unison. The greasy, black, twisted coils never appeared thick enough to support an elevator filled with people of all sizes. I imagined the cables snapping and unwinding in a frantic, out-of-control spin just shy of the fifth-floor landing, sending all the occupants plunging into a wild free-fall to the vast unknown below.

I believed the elevator to be capable of supporting the weight of both my mother and me, plus a few others, but as the crowd gathered for the ride up I began to worry. As each passenger filed in, the cage swayed to and fro. The movement never ceased during the slow, agonizing ascent.

The brown paneled walls in the dental office added to my own general feeling of dread and apprehension. Dr. Moore often acted as his own secretary and busied himself with the scheduling book as we arrived for the appointment. The waiting room, stark and devoid of decoration, had a few straight-back chairs and two small tables. One had information concerning the proper care of your teeth. Some copies of my favorite magazine, *Children's Activities*, were scattered about on the second table. This welcome distraction kept me occupied while I waited for my name to be called.

I required assistance getting into the adult-sized brown, cracked leather examination chair. I stretched to rest my head on the two

This picture nearly matches my memory of Dr. Moore's office
(Example of a 1935 dental office from the Melnick Medical Museum)

circular supports. My feet dangled well above the ornate, metal foot rest. The chair faced a floor-to-ceiling window: a scary perch from which to watch the goings-on below on Dorrance Street.

Could the fierce pain of the drill hitting a nerve cause me to fly forward, crashing through the glass window, hurtling hand over foot down onto the busy, congested street below? It seemed a possibility.

I sat rigid with my mouth opened wide as Dr. Moore leaned forward. The smell of the egg salad he consumed on his frequent breaks into the tiny room behind the chair lingered on his breath. The Vitalis combed into his shiny, black, full head of hair produced an overpowering stench of both hair gel and egg. His generous belly growled as the white, spotless, starched jacket crunched under gentle pressure against my ear, making for a strange musical mishmash.

On one such visit Dr. Moore stepped back, smiled, and announced in a booming voice to my mother, "Anita has a perfect bite."

The word *perfect* had never been used in reference to anything I had achieved in my short, young life until now. The words rang though the examining room as if they had been sung by a choir of sweet angels and not the thunderous articulation of Dr. Moore.

Arriving home that afternoon, I discovered that my friends were not around. I asked my mother if I could go down to the very end of Harris Street to play with Peter Marquette. Five-year-old Peter, the youngest and only boy in his family, had two doting older sisters who spoiled him. I don't know why, but I never really liked Peter.

It did not take long for us to engage in a scuffle. We began to push each other. I think the altercation may have been over me wanting to ride his bike. For some reason, known only to God, I grabbed Peter's arm and bit him with my *perfect bite*. He ran screaming into his house. I turned and bolted up the street in the race of my life.

My mother questioned me as I burst through the back door. "What have you been up to?"

"Oh nothing," I replied, trying to catch my breath.

She pressed further, but I divulged no wrong-doing. After a short time my mother happened to walk into the dining room and glance out the window. She spotted Mrs. Marquette with Peter in tow.

"Glory be to Gawd, it's Regina Marquette," my mother cried in horror. What have you done now?"

Everyone feared Mrs. Marquette. As principal at the local elementary school she stood for no nonsense. She was one of those small people who appeared big. I watched, frozen in place, as Mrs. Marquette proceeded up the street marching toward our house with the efficiency and purpose of an entire marching band.

My mother opened the front door and graciously asked them to come in and sit down. They both entered, but did not take a seat. Peter and I hid behind our mothers, saying nothing.

"Yes, Regina. Yes, Regina," was all I recall my mother saying.

In time they left. My punishment, a week in the yard without friends, was a relief considering my wicked, insensitive crime. I do not remember playing with Peter again.

A few years later Dr. Moore left private practice and joined the Navy somewhere in the South Pacific. I was happy he had moved so far away, never to return.

Regina Marquette lived to be one hundred years old. Her alma mater (and mine), Rhode Island College, honored her as a distinguished graduate and the oldest and most active alumna. A photograph of Mrs. Marquette on the front page of the college newspaper showed a woman looking not much different to me than the person I encountered one distressing afternoon many decades earlier.

Age did not camouflage her steely gaze, riveting right through the photograph at me: *the child biter with the perfect bite.* I glanced at the photograph for only a moment, then quickly turned the page.

A MATTER OF CONSCIENCE
Scary Stuff

"Little girl, come here," the old man shouted.

I heard him call, but didn't pay any attention. I was busy leaning over the railing on the Turner Avenue bridge looking down at the water below tumbling and rushing haphazardly over the rocks.

The edge of the protective barrier dug into me as I bent further forward mesmerized by the activity below. Going back to school after lunch I often found time to dawdle at this favorite spot. I tossed a stick into the water then ran across the street to watch as it appeared from beneath the underpass bobbing and twisting, wending its way downstream. It would not take long for my little stick to conclude its journey at the huge, steel, corrugated culvert under the next street.

I was lost in my thoughts, yet also aware that my fourth-grade teacher, Sister Killian, would be waiting at the classroom door, stern faced, and ready to inquire about my tardiness.

I dropped another stick over the railing and watched as it floated in the air then caught on the stream bank momentarily, before dislodging itself under the water's relentless force. Again, I darted across the street to view the small twig skip and dip as it exited below. It would have been fun to run along the well-worn foot path that followed the brook all the way to Fenner Avenue, but I knew better.

I crossed Turner Avenue one more time to repeat my game using a heavier stick. The voice called a second time.

"Little girl, little girl, come here."

I saw the old man on the other side of the swamp, a short distance away, standing in his front yard beckoning to me. This nameless man could often be seen digging in the small garden behind his house. His clothes, too large for his slight frame, made him appear disheveled as he waved his arms in my direction.

I had walked by his home numerous times on my way to school. Sometimes I went the Turner Avenue route, but more often with the possibility of being late for school, the brook shortcut made sense.

When taking the route through the brook, there were rules you observed. If it was foggy, rainy, dark, or you saw boys hanging out at the foot bridge, you chose the longer way, Turner Avenue.

The narrow dirt path through the swamp ran along a barrier of tall weeds, cattails, and pools of water where all sorts of pond creatures lurked: snakes, skunks, box turtles, muskrats, and bull frogs as big as a man's fist. Danger and suspense of the unknown accompanied you every step of the way.

The old man's house, a tiny, one-story structure with a center front door framed by two windows stood right beyond the foot bridge. The outside walls, encased in red brick siding, resembled roofing, appearing granular, rough, and uneven. The neighborhood kids referred to his house as *the shack*.

He called a third time.

"Come here."

I felt safe against the railing and did wonder if he needed help, but just the same, he frightened me.

Was he sick? Did he need a doctor? Had he run out of bread or did he want only to talk with someone?

It would take just a few minutes for me to get closer and shout to him from a safe distance, but I could hear my mother's admonition ringing in my ears.

"Keep going when you pass the old man's house. Do not stop."

My mother liked us to help others, but deep in my heart I knew that assisting this stranger seemed to be in direct conflict concerning her lessons on neighborliness.

Her rules were few, but chiseled in stone with the permanence and authority of the Ten Commandments. We seldom questioned them and I believe we were relieved to have some restrictions on our activities

His plea went unanswered. I turned in the direction of school and ran as fast as my legs would carry me, past the McPherson's, Dr. Green's, the pretty yellow house set behind the stone wall, the nun's convent, the church, the rectory, and at last to the safety behind the school's chain-link fence. Sister Killian looked my way, but said nothing.

I did not pay attention to any of my lessons that afternoon. My thoughts were crowded with conflict, self-inflicted guilt, and unanswered questions.

I walked along Turner Avenue at the end of the school day and glanced toward his house. He was nowhere to be seen.

I did not tell my mother of my scary confrontation because I knew that she would never let me go to the brook again. I kept the secret to myself.

A few days later Mary and I cut through the swamp on our way to school. The old man's house appeared abandoned. The front door was closed shut and he was not working in his garden. The old man was gone.

"He would be out weeding his garden now if I had helped him," I sometimes thought as I passed his house.

Was he dead because I did not divulge my dark secret to Sister Killian or my mother? Am I to blame? Did my inaction contribute to some calamity?

My single consolation was only that I did obey my mother.

My friends did not discuss his possible whereabouts or, I don't think, were even aware that he was no longer there. I stayed with my dismal secret for a while, and, like most children, went on to other things and forgot about the incident, yet here I am today remembering and writing about what took place so many, many years ago.

"Little girl, little girl, come here."

LONDON BRITCHES FALLING DOWN

Slippery Stuff

I could feel it slipping and sliding, moving with willful determination inside its fabric casing, like a small snake slithering through the grass. It followed the insignificant curves of my six-year-old waistline. I realized in an instant that a possible life-altering event was unfolding. The elastic holding my stunning flesh-colored satin McQuiggin underpants had detached from its moorings.

These were not just any ordinary underpants. They had two large magnificent lace bows sewed flat on both sides. Each lace-trimmed leg flared out, reminiscent of a tap-dancing outfit that Ginger Rogers might have worn while circling the dance floor with Fred Astaire. They were exquisite.

This was not the first time a McQuiggin article of clothing had given me trouble. I loved the maroon taffeta skirt with the shirred waist that I pulled from one of the boxes mailed to us. It fit me to perfection. My mother had sewed me a white, batiste peasant blouse that looked like it had been custom made for that skirt.

One day walking home from school for lunch, I lingered behind everyone so I could spin down Turner Avenue on the narrow, packed dirt sidewalk in my crisp taffeta outfit. Checking first to see that my friends were well on their way home and out of sight, I began to twirl around and around, watching with pleasure as my skirt ballooned out. I remember seeing the telephone pole coming toward me, but that is all I recall. I did not know how much time had passed before I became aware of my surroundings. I found myself gripping the mailbox a short distance from the pole. A quick glance up and down the street revealed everyone had vanished. The street was empty. My concern was not that I may have rendered myself unconscious, but if anyone had seen me collide with the pole. I looked briefly across the street at Dr. Smith's office. I felt a wave of reassurance he was close by. Steadying myself, I walked home for lunch, feeling off-balance and a bit queasy.

Now, I was experiencing a second McQuiggin clothing incident of a more serious nature.

Having finished with the afternoon reading group, we all returned to our seats. At this very moment my underpants drama began. Sister Mary Esperance, my young chubby-faced teacher, told us to put our books away and line up for recess. I fought off panic and dug my elbows into my waist in a desperate attempt to keep the faulty underpants from sliding to the ground. Following my classmates out to the school yard, I walked over and leaned against the side of the building, hoping no one would ask me to play a game. This did not happen.

"Hey, Nita, we need you for Red Rover," yelled my best friend, Barbara.

"No, I don't feel like it," I shouted back.

Usually Barbara's reaction to a response like that would be to run over, grab my arm, and pull me into the game but, for some reason, she did not. I took my first deep, relaxing breath.

Following recess we rested, heads down, at our desks. My arms began to ache as I continued to clench my waistline to avoid the disaster of having the swishy, satin underpants plummet to the floor with the speed and accuracy of the Lone Ranger's silver bullet.

I knew the time had come. I cautiously raised my hand. Sister Esperance extended her long, tapered index finger and beckoned me to her desk. I pressed my elbows in deeper and walked up to her desk. I leaned into her to where I imagined her ear might be located under layers of black veiling, divulging my secret. Again, without uttering a word, she pointed her finger in the direction of the cloakroom.

I entered and waited. Sister slipped in, like most nuns did, in silence and with the grace of a dancer. She smiled the smile of the angels. For a fleeting moment in time Sister Esperance became my best friend, my big sister, my mother, but not my first-grade teacher. Sister whispered that I should lift my skirt and she would tighten and pin the offending elastic band in place. She raised her stiff white bib. It looked as if she knew a crisis would be on her agenda this traumatic Monday afternoon. She was ready. An amazing plethora of common pins and safety pins of varying sizes adorned a never-seen-before chest area of her black habit. Her cool, smooth hands pulled the beautiful satin pants firmly around my waist and she secured the errant elastic with a safety pin.

"There, Anita, this will hold everything secure until you get home."

With those reassuring words I confidently returned to my seat.

My mother repaired my fancy satin underpants and on following Monday washday they arrived back in my drawer. I never wore them again, dreading this harrowing event just might repeat itself, but it was enjoyable having them around. I laid the flesh-colored satin undergarment alongside my sensible Sears and Roebuck waffle-weave "snuggies," affording me the opportunity for a quick loving glance at the fancy, slippery McQuiggin underpants every morning.

Some things in life, no matter how much you love and cherish them, just exude danger and keep you from ever giving them a second chance.

IN VOGUE

A Slippery Slope

No question about it, my lovely satin underpants were a thing of beauty. The two delicate lace bows adorning each side added richness and refinement.

The previous story recalls how this fancy undergarment came dangerously close to ruining my young first-grade life had it not been for the quick thinking and kindness of Sister Mary Esperance, RSM.

God bless her!

MRS. KEMPT

Bad Manners

A sense of utmost urgency gripped my sister, Mary, and me as we hurried to complete our Saturday morning household chores.

"You forgot a little spot under that dining room chair," my mother reprimanded.

We had to get to our friend, Lianne's, house now or we could miss everything.

As soon as our jobs passed parental inspection, Mary and I jumped on our bikes and peddled around the corner to Lianne's house. We dropped our bikes on her front lawn, ran up the porch steps, while knocking in unison on the wooden screen door. Mrs. Kempt, Lianne's grandmother, invited us to come in and sit at the kitchen table while we waited for our friend.

Our friend, Lianne, 1946

Mrs. Kempt, a no-nonsense, unsmiling, gray-haired, petite woman appeared ancient to nine- and ten-year-old kids. We sat in silence watching her every move. She put a tea bag into her cup and shuffled over to the stove in her flat, well-worn, maroon felt slippers. Mrs. Kempt then turned the gas off under the whistling kettle and poured the boiling water into her cup.

Was this her second cup? Were we too late?

To our delight, Mrs. Kempt retrieved a piece of burnt toast from the toaster. It appeared curved and must have been in the slot for some time. We were in luck. She had not eaten her breakfast.

Her everyday act of eating seemed just extraordinary to us. Mrs. Kempt was about to devour her dry, well-done toast without the aid of a single tooth. This fascinating process demanded our complete attention. We thought ourselves to be invisible observers as she opened her mouth and inserted the toast. She drew it in and clasped the toast between her toothless upper and lower gums, firmly holding it all in place. Our eyes were riveted on the scene before us.

With a quick downward thrust, she snapped off one corner. Her lower jaw began to rotate in rhythmic fashion, gradually widening in a clockwise direction. The skin around her lips formed elongated grooves, continually changing as her jaw performed this repetitive, circular journey. We watched, mesmerized, sitting rigid in our chairs.

Mrs. Kempt took a sip of tea. She waited for a moment, then swallowed. Mary and I prepared ourselves for the next chew. Without shame, we brazenly sat there gawking at Lianne's grandmother as she continued to consume her meager breakfast.

My sister and I learned all about proper manners as children, but not to brazenly stare at a toothless grandmother as she ate her morning meal appeared to be the one lesson in etiquette my mother had not yet covered.

THE FACTS OF LIFE

I Am a Big Girl Now

I had never heard of that expression, Facts of Life, at the tender age of five or six, but I was about to discover that the mysteries of life were just that: mysterious.

I had several dolls that were lots of fun, especially my Ideal Wet-me-Wet. This eight-inch, nameless doll kept me occupied for hours. I never tired of dressing and undressing my small friend. I could bathe her all-rubber body in the bassinette that I begged for one Christmas and received. Another Christmas I found a metal black-and-white checkered doll's trunk with a latch and key that proved to be effective in keeping my sister, Mary, away from my doll's precious possessions. Inside this spacious suitcase, I discovered coat hangers, a mirror, a shelf, and two drawers with small round brass knobs. A handle on top made it a portable item to carry to the homes of my friends.

My good friend, Lianne, who was a few years older than me, also liked to play dolls.

Lianne was different from most of the neighborhood kids. She had a daring edge to her. She took chances, made you laugh, had no trouble being bad in the standard of the 1940s, and always had an idea in her head, theorizing the next activity. She was afraid of no one. I admired her toughness and, as I discovered one afternoon, her worldliness.

The phone rang. It was Lianne.

"Nita, come on over to my house and we will play dolls."

"Okay, let me ask my mother."

"Sure, you can go, Anita, but remember to walk on the sidewalk."

Lianne's house was only around the corner, but my mother liked to bestow a departing order or two. She forgot our street did not have sidewalks, but Lianne's did.

I climbed the slight incline up to her side yard. She was sitting cross-legged in a school dress under the apple tree next to the empty lot that adjoined Grandmother Westfield's yard. We often wore dresses year-round. Slacks and shorts were mostly for going to camp or when the fall weather began to turn cool.

The old apple tree with its low hanging branches provided us with privacy and protection from the sun. If Fuffa and Pee Wee, the neighborhood boys, happened to walk by and saw us playing dolls, they may have called out that we were babies. Cowboys and Indians were okay, but not dolls.

"It's past lunchtime, Nita, we better feed our dolls."

I opened my checkered trunk and took out my rubber doll and her little baby bottle, then ran over to the hose attached to the side of the house. I filled it, drip by drip, and ran back across the grass. I positioned the elongated orange nipple on the mouth of the bottle and pulled it around the opening.

Lianne picked up her doll and held her against the bodice of her print flowered cotton dress.

"Lianne, where is your baby's bottle? Did you leave it in the house?"

Lianne laughed at me. She said nothing.

I repeated my questions as she pulled her doll closer to her upper body, looking down at it with a new-found affection as if she liked her baby doll more than she did me.

My friend waited then, with an air of disgust, looked up from her task and snapped at me,

"I AM feeding my doll. I am giving her milk from me. I'm breastfeeding."

I did not know what she was talking about. I began to question Lianne, eager for her to impart every bit of information she was privy to about feeding her doll in this new and exciting secret way. She proclaimed that she had no intention of ever using a baby bottle again.

Lianne continued giving her doll lunch, looking smug and pleased with herself. I cast my eyes down and gave my Wet-me-Wet the remainder of her bottle. I felt the warm trickle of the doll's watery lunch roll down my leg and into my socks. I remained quiet then told Lianne my mother would be ringing the bell for me to go home soon. I packed up my baby gear and left.

I never questioned my mother about my startling, spanking-new information. I wondered if she knew about it.

A few years later my mother gave birth to my beautiful baby sister, Alicia Catherine. I watched her sitting on the sofa discretely feeding Alicia under a small blanket not quite large enough to cover my mother's exposed, bare shoulder. She said the baby was getting milk from her. I watched with unparalleled curiosity. I waited in vain for the blanket to slip so as to get a full view of the proceedings, but it never happened.

I realized that Lianne, for all her bravado, did not have the whole process of breastfeeding down to an exact science. Listening to my little sister's gentle sucking noises, I concluded that you could not feed your baby doll through the fabric of your summer cotton dress.

For the time being, breastfeeding was all I needed to know about the Facts-of-Life. I continued to ride my bike, play cowboys and Indians, and roller-skate up and down our smooth cement driveway with my metal, clip-on skates.

I still liked playing with my Ideal Wet-me-Wet doll. I lovingly cradled her close to my chest, as she enjoyed a lunch of water from her tiny, glass baby bottle.

IN VOGUE

Fashion Perfection

A while back I noticed a peasant blouse featured in a glossy fashion magazine. It resembled one my mother sewed for me when I was in the third grade.

My soft white cotton batiste blouse was flawless. The front bow gently drew the neckline in slightly below my neck, giving a very feminine appearance. The cuffs on the sleeves, gathered with an elastic thread drawn through a casing, made a dainty gathering just above my wrists.

My dad took a portrait of me in this beautiful top one Sunday afternoon in his photography studio in our basement.

THE WISHING WELL

Heart's Desire

Wish #1: __Horse Tales__

I dreamed of getting a horse, as did my sister, Mary. We had a double garage and only one car, so space did not seem to be an issue of where to build the horse stall. We promised my mother the grooming, feeding, and exercising would be our responsibility. She listened, smiled, and went about her work.

We had experience with horses. Mr. Goff, a man who lived in the country a mile or so beyond our house, owned a pony that pulled a bouncy, rattan, two-wheeled cart. His pony, sprightly and lively, moved as if to the beat of a base drum. Sometimes on Sundays he took his favorite kids from our neighborhood for a ride around the block, one by one. I was never chosen, but I always stood waiting, hoping to be next.

I considered Claire Sandstrum a friend, even though I did not play

199

with her. I think her horse, Betty, must have taken up most of her time. She lived a few doors up from Mr. Goff on Forbes Street. Once or twice a summer Claire appeared atop her horse in front of Lianne's house. A small group of children stood around stroking Betty's smooth, brown coat and begging Claire for a ride.

"You can ride to the Villeneuve's house, turn around, and then come back right here for a nickel," exclaimed Claire.

Neither Mary nor I ever had change in our pockets, so we ran home to get the money for a ride. Claire assisted us in getting our feet into the stirrups and showed everyone the correct way to grasp the reins. She held on to the horse's bridle and Betty clomped down the street and back at a pace just shy of a standstill.

And there were other horses. Once during the summer, Mike-the-Ragman, arrived in our neighborhood. He could be heard yelling,

"Rags. Rags."

I think every kid in the neighborhood who heard his cry came running to view this strange fellow and his horse. His cart was piled high with a jumble of rags. He appeared old with grey hair and wrinkled skin. Mike-the-Ragman sat on a raised wooden seat with shoulders stooped, leaning forward and grasping the worn, curled, soiled leather reigns.

The sleepy, dusty old horse pulled his master and the goods down the street. They paused a moment or two in front of a few houses. He yelled again and again, but no one came outside to engage in business with him.

The boys in the neighborhood teased Mike-the-Ragman, jumping up and down alongside his horse and echoing the rag man's call. He never said a word but, with the boys' taunting, flicked the reigns on the horse's backside and vanished around the corner heading in the direction of the main road. We didn't see Mike-the-Ragman and his horse for another year.

One Christmas morning my mother asked Mary and me to open

two identically wrapped boxes at the same time. We tore the holiday wrapping off our gifts and discovered a box of writing stationery featuring a colorful painting of a horse in the upper right corner. Each sheet was illustrated with a different horse.

"Well girls, there is your horse," laughed my mother.

We, too, found this funny, because we knew getting a horse to be out of the question. I examined each piece of paper and decided that I wanted to keep my beautiful horse stationery in perfect condition. This did not happen. The day after Christmas we engaged in the annual routine: thank you notes. Gradually with each correspondence, my attractive stationery vanished horse by handsome horse.

Wish #2: <u>A Bike by Any Other Name</u>

Eventually a skinny-tire Raleigh English bike did enter my life: not under the tree at Christmas, but one I purchased with my own money.

When I began teaching the second grade, I needed transportation to school. I could not afford a car on my meager salary, so a bike would have to do.

I put an ad in the *Barrington Times*, a local newspaper. I felt if I could find a Raleigh anyplace it would be in the affluent town of

Barrington. I received a response the first week my ad ran from a Mrs. Fraiser who said her daughter was going off to college and no longer needed her Raleigh. It even had a distinctive *F* painted on the rear fender. I rode my $35 acquisition every day to school, rain or shine, and on most days with several second graders peddling along behind me.

For the two summers I attended college in Boston. I rode my bike every day to my classes. I loved dodging traffic and beating the cars traveling my daily route down Commonwealth Avenue. It did not take me long to learn that you do not lock your bike overnight to the fence in front of your apartment while you are upstairs sleeping. Each night something vanished from my beloved Raleigh. First my leather tool kit disappeared, then the basket. Finally when the pump went missing, it was time to put my beautiful English bike in the cellar. I lugged it up the steep stairs of the brownstone in the morning and down the unlit, narrow stairway in the afternoon.

In time I married and we moved often. Caring for a family of six, I rode my bike less and less. One day a friend asked me if I wanted to put anything in her garage sale.

"Yes, I have one thing," I told her.

I struggled to get my Raleigh in the back of the car and then drove out to her home. I printed $15 on an index card and taped it to the handlebars. An older man stopped his car and walked down the gravel driveway to the sale. He examined my treasured bike and handed me $15. I watched him push the bike up the incline of the driveway. I began to cry. He heard my sobs and turned around.

"That's okay. You can have it back," he yelled down to me.

"No. It's yours. I don't use it anymore."

He drove off.

Every time I catch sight of a three-speed, skinny-tire Raleigh in my village, I look to see if it happens to be my much-loved bike. So far, a bicycle with its identifiable *F* on the rear fender, has eluded me.

Wish #3: <u>*Baby Boomer*</u>

For years my older sister, Mary, and I begged my mother for a baby. We had no idea how this was accomplished, but we thought a baby would be fun. My mother looked at us, smiled, and usually murmured,

"We'll see."

Time went by and no baby. We tired of forever reminding our mother about our request and in time just gave up.

One day my mother gathered us together and said,

"Remember that baby you used to ask for? Well, you are going to get a new sister or brother in June."

This great news was beyond anything we could imagine.

The day the baby was due home from the hospital Mary and I sat on the front porch swing with my Aunt Alice. The waiting for this monumental event was interminable.

By mid-afternoon my dad's car turned into the driveway with our neighbor, Mrs. Gill, holding our brand-new sister in the front seat. My mother sat alone in the back.

After the excitement of the day died down Mary and I went up to our room for the night. We began to talk things over. We were annoyed with Mrs. Gill for sitting there in the front all the while glancing down lovingly and holding the baby wrapped cozy and snug against her chest. My mother and our new little sister belonged sitting up front next to my father. We both agreed that Mrs. Gill had nudged in a little too close to our family circle that day.

Wish #4: <u>Keeping Up With the Times</u>

My final wish took the longest of all. I wanted a television.

My friend, Barbara, had one, as did the Whitakers down the road, and best of all, so did the Overdeeps across the street.

I never missed *I Remember Momma*. I boldly knocked on the Overdeep's front door at eight o'clock sharp on Friday evenings. I had no shame. I wasn't invited and never asked if I could drop by. I just showed up.

They welcomed me in, and we all sat in silence and watched

the story line unfold. Maxwell House commercials, as well as the program itself, contributed to our evening entertainment. For a half hour we remained transfixed and captivated, observing the mundane lives of Momma, Papa, Nels, and Dagmar.

Our neighbors, the Whitakers, had a television. They lived across the street from the Monkey Lady. No one knew them very well, so going up to their door and expecting to be invited inside was not in the realm of possibility.

Before the street lights came on as a signal for all kids to go home, we stood leaning against a telephone pole directly across the street from the Whitakers' living room windows. In time we got bolder and walked into their front yard. Our small gang of interlopers hid in their shrubbery elbowing each other to get a better view of the silent picture at the far end of the room. We engaged in this rude, peeping-Tom caper as often as we dared. Once we watched as Mr. Whitaker got up from his chair. We thought he was going into the kitchen, but no, he threw open the front door and roared in a voice loud enough for all of us to hear.

"Get out of here, all of you. Go home."

Frightened that we had been discovered but worse, possibly identified, we scattered as fast as our legs would carry us in every direction, never to return.

My father's initial argument for not buying a television was that he thought it best to wait until we were able to receive on-the-spot, live programming. My guess is that eventually this did happen or that my father just wanted a television.

He built a mahogany turntable on top of an old wind-up Victrola cabinet with two shelves below for our 45" record player and Zenith radio we had received for Christmas.

The entire family gathered around in anticipation as my father slit open the cardboard packing box and lifted our new television up on to the table. We all squealed in excitement but, to my horror, it did not have a wood finish but was made of pink metal. Our longed-for television sat atop the shiny mahogany stand sporting not one, but two shades of pink. No one I knew owned a pink television but us.

I recall my little sister, Alicia, sitting cross-legged under the arch between the dining room and living room with her Mickey Mouse ears clipped to her head. She sang along with the entire ensemble of Mouseketeers:

"*M-I-C------K-E-Y------M-O-U-S-E*"

Alicia gazed at the television transfixed as Darlene, Bobby, and Annette danced and twirled across our twelve-inch, two-tone pink metal Motorola television screen.

I can almost hear my dad's laughter as each week he regaled in the humor of Jack Benny and his sidekick, Mr. Rochester.

My mother challenged herself by tuning in to her beloved show, *Concentration*, featuring a variety of hosts, her favorite being Hugh Downs. The entire family enjoyed the clever questioning from the panel of *What's My Line*. As for me, I would watch anything my parents would allow.

I learned that the waiting, the getting, or the not getting were all a part of the growing-up process, and like most kids of my generation, there was plenty of waiting.

DOWN UNDER

Forbidden Territory

"Ann—nee—ta, stay away from the Floyd's house."

My mother's occasional stern demeanor meant only one thing: obey. She had several of these one-liners that were not to be crossed. My undivided attention to the matter at hand did not mean I would follow with blind obedience, but it caused me to ponder and aroused a curiosity that I found difficult to resist. What did my mother know that I did not? It was as if she had handed her young daughter an invitation to adventure.

The Floyds were a strange family, mostly because we knew almost nothing about them. They kept to themselves.

They lived on a low piece of land that appeared to hug the stone wall at the far end of Lianne's backyard. Their small, white, unattractive, one-story, cottage-type home faced the brook: a magnificent wild play area enjoyed by every kid in the neighborhood. From their front porch they had an unobstructed view of marshes, cattails, waterways, and a jungle of trees and bushes. You could not quite tell where their street ended and the Floyd's dirt driveway began. They seemed to melt into one another. A small stream meandered

Mary and me
posing at the Good's apple tree

207

from under the far end of their porch and headed in the direction of the swamp. It vanished into the dark, thick, vegetation at the very edge of the marsh.

I often walked by their house along the path to take the shortcut over the wooden foot bridge at the brook on my way to school. On occasion I saw Mr. Floyd, a small, muscular man with a pot belly going about his business in the yard. Occasionally, I'd see Mrs. Floyd, a short woman, always in a house dress and apron, standing on the porch leaning against the railing with a broom in her hand staring in the direction of the brook, all the while chatting with Mr. Floyd. They never spoke to me nor did I talk with them. I knew their youngest son, Joe, because he played with my friend Patty's older brother, Sunny. Joe had one other brother. I spotted him occasionally standing on the porch.

We loved to play on the swing that Lianne's dad, Mr. Good, hung from a sturdy branch on the sizable apple tree in her backyard. The swing faced the side of the Floyd's house.

The sun shone brightly on this cool late fall afternoon. We all had on our best church coats and hats and decided it might be fun to play on the swing before we were summoned to go home for Sunday dinner. My mother rang a bell for us that we were able to hear all the way to Lianne's.

"Push me higher! Push me higher!" was the ongoing cry of the one lucky enough to be sitting on the swing.

Sometimes we went so high in the air that the rope hopped, making us think that there was a possibility of flying off and landing on the Floyd's roof.

Usually, at this point in the commotion, the expected happened. Mrs. Floyd magically appeared at the stone wall shaking her finger at us,

"Stop that noise. Get out of here. Don't you know my boy fell off a train and needs his rest?"

I thought Mr. and Mrs. Floyd's son must not have had too much common sense. I pictured him standing atop a speeding train, his legs spread apart, arms thrust toward the sky, laughing to his heart's content enjoying his wild train ride. Then, without warning, the train jerked, he lost his balance, and dropped with a thud to the gravel below. It did not occur to me that he may have tumbled while working on a welding repair job on the roof of a detached boxcar off on a spur in a railyard.

That was all Mrs. Floyd said and then she would vanish into the house, but we felt her eyes riveted on us watching our activities from a window. At times we could even see her shadow through the curtains.

In defiance, we always departed after a few more pushes, since it was Lianne's yard and her swing and only our mothers, we felt, could give us orders, not Mrs. Floyd.

We soon tired of swinging and had not heard the bell to call us home, so we had time to do something else. Lianne never ran out of suggestions.

"Hey, let's walk by Floyd's. There were no cars in the yard when I went by their house after church."

We stood on Burnside Avenue and looked over at their driveway. Lianne was right – no cars.

"Let's go check on the stream in their yard." Mary and I dutifully followed.

We stood at the edge of the long ditch and peered down. It did not look like anything we had seen before. The brown water appeared thick and murky and uneven. It didn't move.

"Hey, I'm going to jump over it," shouted Lianne.

She took one step back and then leaped and landed on the opposite side with the accuracy of a young mountain goat.

"Look out, I'm going over too," exclaimed Mary.

Mary hit the lip of the embankment on the opposite side. She dug her fingers into the mud, fought to gain her balance, and barely made a safe landing.

"I'm going to jump," I announced.

"You're too little and too fat," proclaimed Lianne.

She made me so mad that I didn't even back up for a running start.

"No, don't, don't," warned Mary. "You won't make it."

I jumped, almost knowing I was destined for immediate failure. I landed in the middle of the brown quagmire. I hit the dense, syrupy mess like a rock dropped into a vat of molasses. As soon as my shoes broke the surface, a rancid, putrid smell pierced the air.

"It's their cesspool," screamed Lianne.

I continued to sink slowly, wiggling in every direction as my feet searched for solid footing. The sewage slowly made contact with the point of the velvet collar on my fashionable McQuiggin coat.

Lianne fell to the ground along the edge of the embankment. She grabbed me by the shoulder of my coat and pulled and yanked, never letting go. She continued struggling while yelling orders for to me force myself over to the side of the bank. Mary laid down beside Lianne and they both tugged and pulled at me until I was able to wiggle up the slimy edge of the embankment. We all began to scream and I started to cry as loud as I could. Lianne held one shoulder of my disgraced coat and Mary held the other as they walked me home. They each pinched their nose shut with their free hand.

By the time we could see my house, we noticed my mother walking at a fast clip toward us.

"I could hear the racket inside the house," she exclaimed. She could not believe what was before her. She said her usual:

"Glory be to Gawd, Anita, what did you do now?"

"She fell into Floyd's sewer," chimed Mary and Lianne.

"I told you two to stay away from that place. It's a wonder you didn't drown. Get to the back door. Lianne you had better go home."

"Mary, go in the house. I want you to take a bath."

My mother stripped off most of my clothing. I stood in my underwear, still crying, as she gave my dress, hat, and coat a mighty toss into the backyard. I imagined every neighbor peering out their window in amazement, wondering why I was standing almost naked in my underpants on our back steps this cool afternoon.

Alarmed by my screaming, my father arrived at the back door. He told me to go to the cellar and wait. He soon came down the stairs with an enamel tub partially filled with warm, soapy water. He looked away as he attempted to wash his wayward child standing in a tub on his workbench. He quickly wrapped a beach towel around my bare body and sent me upstairs to my mother for a second bath.

"I told you not to go to Floyd's and you disobeyed. You are in the yard every day after school for a week."

I felt relieved to receive my punishment. I deserved it and maybe more. I said nothing.

My father cleaned the foul-smelling area on his workbench, then went out to the backyard. He walked over to the garage, fetched a shovel, and began to dig. He quickly deposited all my offensive clothing in the hole. My father then covered it with dirt, sprinkled some grass seed on the fresh soil, and raked it over.

Mary went to Lianne's after school on Monday. Mrs. Good answered the door.

"Lianne can't play; she is being punished for going to Floyd's."

"Lianne didn't push Nita into the sewer, Mrs. Good."

"Yes, but I am very sure that it was her idea to go to there in the first place and then jump over the stream."

Mary nodded her head and walked home.

The indignity of falling into a cesspool did make an impression on me and I began to do what I was told more often.

My mother's directives kept coming, but not too often, since she chose her marching orders with care, giving credence only to what she considered to be of grave importance.

Me, Lianne, and Mary, October, 1943
Picture taken prior to our forbidden adventure

THE O'ROURKES

Unsolved Mystery

You didn't mess with the O'Rourkes.

The O'Rourke kids lived on Read Street just before you turned off onto a gravel road that led into Little Neck Cemetery. This seemed an appropriate location because they were a scary bunch. Everyone gave them plenty of room.

There were several children in the family. They wielded power and instilled fear in the hearts of many. We didn't play with them, but we observed. Their house was a short bike ride from my neighborhood.

"Stay away from the O'Rourkes." These words of warning were rarely spoken but practiced just the same.

Their two-story square house, never fully completed, added another dimension to their rough and tumble lives. The yard, a large area of well-packed dirt, made a good place for them to play. A tall tree in the back went beyond the singular function of providing shade.

A thick rope attached to a sturdy branch sported a fat knot on the end. Everyone knew the function of the rope. On occasion, we were told, it was secured in the grip of a closed second-story window as a means of escape if the police happened to be banging on the front door looking for one of them. A high rounded mound of dirt, just beyond the reach of the tree branches, made for a handy landing pad that assisted the escapist in achieving a running start. It remained a mystery how they knew when to put the rope in the ready position.

I never had the privilege of seeing this drama unfold. When passing by the O'Rourkes, a quick sideways glace offered a clear view of the rope. You never went alone down Read Street. The security of a friend remained imperative.

When biking by their house on the way to check out the graves at mysterious and secluded Little Neck Cemetery, sometimes one of them could be seen hanging out an open window facing the street just staring at the passersby.

"What are YOU looking at?" This inquiry forced you to increase your speed, look straight ahead, and just keep peddling.

I knew only three in the family. Jimmy was in my grade, Jane O'Rourke was my sister Mary's age, and Doreen was the oldest and guardian of the group. Jimmy looked like most boys in my third-grade class: a thin frame, shiny gabardine pants held up by a too-wide belt, and brown, straight hair in need of a cut. Jane was pretty and very slender with straight brown hair to her shoulders. She always wore a dress with sleeves in accordance with St. Brendan's unwritten dress code. Doreen gave off an air of supreme authority. Everyone stayed their distance and never mingled with Doreen. She was the boss.

I was in the third grade and Mary, my sister, in the fourth grade when we shared a classroom with Sister Mary Killian at the helm. This young, pretty, strict, no-nonsense nun kept us mostly in check, but she met her match with Jane O'Rourke.

One day Jane did something that displeased Sister Killian. Jane started to run. Wasting no time, Sister Killian began chasing her around the classroom. Sister Killian, with her veils flying, giant rosary beads hooked at the waist clattering on every desk, ran full tilt as she attempted to seize the back of Jane's dress. She missed. Jane, younger, quicker, and more agile, grabbed the iron center support pole in the middle of the classroom and shimmied up to the ceiling. Sister Killian glanced up at her and may have smiled. She said nothing, walked away and, without comment, continued teaching. Jane stayed up there against the ceiling with her skinny legs and arms wrapped around the pole for some time. Eventually, she slid down and went to her seat without further incident.

Today she would have been treated by the school psychologist. This thrilling episode of daring has remained for my sister Mary and me one of the most exciting days that ever took place at St. Brendan's School. Mary said that she felt Sister Killian and Jane O'Rourke were kindred souls.

Jimmy bunked school often. Bunking, or playing hooky, represented the most serious of school crimes that brought out the town truant officer to handle the situation, along with a member of the local police. Maybe Jimmy engaged in other wrongdoings, but I only remember him being absent from school on a regular basis. In the standard of the 1940s and 50s, that was considered a major offense.

One blustery February afternoon while home from school with a cold, I sat staring out the living room window watching the snow fall.

Suddenly, a boy came running down my street, his brown leather shoes slipping and sliding on the snow-packed road. *Jimmy O'Rourke!* He turned and glanced back, then darted between Mr. Overdeep's two tall hedges across the street. He vanished into the yard behind the dense privet. Seconds later, a white car traveling at a snail's pace entered my street. Large black letters along the side of the car, reaching from front to back, spelled out the word POLICE.

"Run, Jimmy, run!" I called, barely containing myself.

Jimmy, hidden by the snowy hedge, made an exit somewhere in the yard. Within minutes the police car retraced its journey up the road. The rear seat in the squad car was empty. Clever Jimmy had out-foxed the police.

My mother knew Mrs. O'Rourke enough to exchange pleasantries. On one of my mother's frequent trips to the corner grocery store she met Mrs. O'Rourke. My mother noticed that she had a very tiny baby wrapped in a blanket in the grocery cart.

"What a lovely baby," my mother cooed.

Mrs. O'Rourke matter-of-factly said that she was just off the Providence bus after having the baby several days before at the hospital. She thought that it would be wise to pick up a few things at the grocery store before walking home. My mother, in an uncharacteristic loss for words, nodded and again offered her congratulations. I think that afternoon my mother wished, more than any other time in her life, that she had learned to drive the family car.

The O'Rourkes had the unmerited reputation of being the bad kids of Riverside. They talked rough and loud causing you to back away. I think they were smart kids, not a poor family, but just disorganized, clannish, and on the defense for some reason. Doreen, their surrogate mother and warden, managed to keep all her brothers and sisters under the shadow of her broad, protective wings. They remained a mystery.

Thinking back, it might have been fun having Jane O'Rourke as a friend. I never accomplished climbing up a rope, hand over hand, in gym class. Witnessing her aptitude at scooting up a metal pole in elementary school, she may have had no trouble teaching me the tricks of scaling a rope and maybe, before descending, victoriously tagging the gym ceiling.

POTTY TRAINING

Near Death Experience

The Veteran's Memorial Parkway ran along the water making for a pleasant, relaxing drive into downtown Providence. From the backseat of my father's car I could see full tankers in the distance sitting low in the water at the Standard Oil loading docks. My attention was diverted for a moment as I noticed someone alongside the road with his thumb extended, hoping to get a ride.

"Oh, it's John Ballard. Stop. He needs a lift," exclaimed my mother.

Mary and I pulled our shoulders back, almost in unison, and lowered our bodies, like a turtle's head retreating into its shell, all in a desperate attempt to vanish into the wooly upholstered backseat of my father's Plymouth. Our car came to a gliding stop. I turned and saw John sprinting toward us.

Mother exited the passenger seat.

"Push over, girls, John can sit in the front with Dad. I will hop in with the three of you."

John was just not any ordinary guy hitching a ride. Mary and I were in early adolescence, but John was a college man. He commuted to Brown after winning an academic scholarship.

Mary and I squeezed together as if we were joined at birth. Mother, in her fluster to get as comfortable as space would allow, gave Alicia a quick shove. In one last monumental push to accommodate herself, my mother's foot slipped. Her shoe hit the mottled grey chipped enamel stubby-handled child-sized potty on the floor. It flew out the open door and hit the ground like a failed missile. The pot began to roll down the incline toward our soon-to-be passenger. It took a wild ride, right then left, with the speed of a hubcap popping off a tire.

I would have welcomed death at that moment, but it failed to materialize. John, looking bewildered, bent down to retrieve the strange grey object rolling toward his feet but, my mother, in an amazing feat of track and agility, sprinted toward him and snatched up the offending wayward container. She hurried back to the car and discretely placed the potty on the floor of the backseat.

"How is your mother, John? I haven't seen the twins lately."

Mary and I sat rigid, continuing to press ourselves further back against the seat, hoping John would fail to remember our presence.

My father spoke, "John, we're headed into Providence. Where can I drop you off? I'll take you right to wherever you need to go."

"Oh, no. He could be going all the way to the other side of the city to have a pizza at one of the Italian restaurants on Federal Hill. Maybe he is meeting another college friend, or even a girl. I want to die," I thought.

John responded, "Thanks, Mr. LeClaire, I am only headed to the Mettacomet Country Club to caddy."

I could feel Mary's tense body relax. The golf club was just up the hill to the right.

"I'll drive you in, John."

"No, the entrance is fine, Mr. LeClaire."

The car stopped and John thanked my father and mother. He turned in our direction.

"Goodbye, girls."

A sense of relief swept over me. John Ballard did not even know our names. We were in luck: just two unidentifiable teenagers and a little sister.

QUICK LICKS
The Chase

"Hurry up, Nita, you are always so slow. Peddle faster," my friend, Barbara, turned her head yelling back to me.

This prodding to catch up with her didn't bother me anymore, like it did when I first got my Columbia fat-tire bike. Barbara received an English, three speed, skinny-tire bike under her tree the year before. Hers cruised right along. I was forever pumping my heart out, three or four bike lengths behind her.

Barbara took a sharp left turn off Turner Avenue and on to Harris Street.

"Nita, get going. I see two nuns way down by Grandmother Westfield's house. They must be on their way to the New England Dairy to get some ice cream.

To encounter the nuns on their occasional Sunday walk during the summer months was always an unexpected, pleasant surprise. We loved the nuns: well, most of them. They glided along in their sturdy, laced-up pumps like they were operated by some secret walking machine. Their bodies, except their hands and faces, were concealed under layers of black, flowing cloth reaching down to their ankles. Yet, with all this gear, they could walk at an amazing speed. This fast pace came in handy when they had to carry a few quarts of ice cream back to their convent, which was some distance away. If they lagged, talking to every kid along the way, like us, the ice cream would surely be melted by the time they got back home.

We could identify the nuns from the back as easily as we could from the front. Tall and lean would be our favorite, Sister Eunice. A short, fat nun bent forward was an easy guess: Sister Rosemarie, the

Sister Eunice, RSM, and Alicia
Easter, 1950

school principal. Sometimes she was cranky and other times pleasant, but most often she asked prying questions about your family, which usually accompanied her good mood phase. I could hear my mother's admonition ringing in my ears, "Now remember, Anita, if someone asks you personal family questions you can say, *I do not know.*"

Times like this my mother shined like a diamond. Imagine, *lying,* I thought, and getting away with it!

"I think its Sister Eunice and Sister Killian," Barbara pronounced in a stage whisper, which was unnecessary since we were more than a full block away. Barbara changed gears and took off. She came up fast behind the tallest sister and skidded her tires to a screeching halt alongside her. They both jumped. Barbara laughed and so did they. Only Barbara, the nuns' favorite kid, could get away with this wild behavior. She lived across the street from them, took piano lessons from Sister Eunice, and just generally hung around the convent. I think in a lot of ways they felt sorry for her. She didn't have many boundaries since Nana Ring, her grandmother, and Boo Boo, her dog, were her main overseers. Her mother and father both worked and weren't around much.

I caught up with the three of them a minute or so later. Barbara was right. It was Sister Eunice and Sister Killian. I liked Sister Killian when she was away from school. I had her for both the third and fourth grades. She was strict and unsmiling but, when I think of it now, Sister Killian taught those two grades in one room all by herself. There were lots of kids, probably sixty in all.

They asked where we were going.

"Err. We are going to buy some ice cream at the dairy, but we have to go home to get our money."

We felt we had sort of lied since we were not even headed in that direction until we saw them. Not telling the truth to your own sister was one thing but shading the truth to a nun was something else altogether. We hopped back on our bikes again and headed to my house.

"Mom, can Barbara and I have some money for ice cream?"

"Oh, I think so. Let me see where I put my purse?"

I can't believe it. How can my mother misplace her pocketbook all the time?

Barbara and I quickly joined in the search.

"Found it!" yelled Barbara. "It was right here under the *Providence Journal*."

"I hear the cones have gone up to thirty-five cents. That's a disgrace. There are so few ingredients in ice cream," fumed my mother.

She emptied her change purse on the kitchen table.

"Let's see, here is seventy cents exactly."

"Thanks! Thanks!"

We both ran out the back door and on to our bikes. Barbara was off and down the street just as I was putting my weight on to the pedal to get a good start.

"Anita, Anita, wait. I think Daddy and I would like an ice cream too. It is so hot today. It will taste good. Let's see. I'll have black raspberry, no make that coffee, and Dad likes maple walnut. Let me get you the rest of the money."

How could my mother do this to me? Doesn't she see that I am in a rush? I can't tell her I want to catch up with the nuns or she will think I want to join the convent some day. Some things you have to keep secret.

My mother took out a two-dollar bill from her purse.

"Here, Anita, now you give me the seventy cents." I shoved my hands into my pocket and fished around for the coins.

"Here, Mom."

She handed me the money.

"Be careful with the change."

I met up with Barbara at the New England Dairy. She was sitting on the top of the picnic table under the shade of the only tree. She was staring down at the water rolling over the rocks in the nearby stream.

"Push over," I said. "They were gone when I got here," bemoaned Barbara. "Sister Eunice and Sister Killian just vanished. How did they get out of here so fast? I didn't even see them on Harris Street on their way back."

"If my mother wasn't so slow, we would have made it. Let's get our ice cream."

We walked up to the girl at the window.

"We want four sugar cones. One coffee, one maple walnut, one vanilla. I bet you want chocolate, right Barbara?"

"Yeh."

"And one chocolate, all medium size."

"Barbara, take my mother's coffee. I'll hold my dad's maple walnut."

We walked over to our bikes and had a fit of laughter knowing that an almost impossible task was in front of us. We got the bikes up, using only our baby fingers, then we put our arms under the handle bars and began our slow journey back to my house, leaning forward, grasping the cones.

Each ice cream was draped in a waxy paper. This helped, in some small way to keep the ice cream from turning into soup on this hot Sunday.

Periodically we would stop to readjust our bikes and take a few quick licks of the ice cream melting and running down our arms.

We arrived at the end of my driveway and my mother came down from the front porch and relieved us of our misery. Just before she reached us we both licked our arms of the delicious tan, chocolate, and cream-colored stripes now dripping off the tips of our elbows. We boldly took a final lick along the rims on both my parent's cones. My mother looked at us and smiled.

"New England Dairy not only has gone up in price, but they are giving a whole new shape to their ice cream cones."

My mother peeled the paper off her coffee and my father's maple walnut. She handed the papers to Barbara and me. Lots of ice cream remained on the surface. We held the paper flat in our free hand. With a few quick licks the coffee and maple walnut bonus treat vanished.

"Thanks," we chimed in unison. "Mom, here's the money."

"Want to exchange one lick each, Barbara?"

"OK, but don't take too much off the top."

"Don't worry, I won't. I'll only take a little because vanilla tastes better than chocolate. Chocolate always makes me thirsty."

Favorites over the years:

Flavors:	Ages:
Vanilla	0-8
Black raspberry	8-9
Raspberry swirl	8-9
Vanilla	9-16
Coffee	16 to present

TOUR DE PAWTUCKET

Journey's End

"It's rich. Anita, it looks so rich on you," exclaimed Mrs. Overdeep.

An invitation by the Overdeeps to Pawtucket seemed like a good idea on the first week of vacation.

The Overdeep's daughter, Florence, needed a new dress and my mother thought a light summer one for the hot, humid days ahead seemed sensible. Something nice, she felt, would cost about $12.

We never shopped in Pawtucket, always Providence with its wide selection of department stores, but going to someplace different looked like fun.

Mr. Overdeep parked the car in the store lot and stayed put, relaxing, readying himself to light up one of his hand-rolled cigarettes. The three of us proceeded to the young girls' department of the New York Lace store.

Mrs. Overdeep held up two dressy dresses that she thought we might like to try on. Florence and I obliged and headed to our own changing stalls and came out ready to model the dresses for approval: both of us attired in fancy lace.

"Turn around, Anita. Lovely. It's beautiful on you, my dear."

A circular turnstile to my left displayed several dresses in my size. One trimmed with daisies around the hem and neckline caught my eye. The daisy dress, the perfect size and style, did not win Mrs. Overdeep's approval, even though Florence liked it.

"It's just too plain for church, my dear. The lacy dress is more appropriate. Your mother would like it."

I didn't think so, but being polite and never wanting to disappoint such a sweet, caring woman as my neighbor, I bought the fancy dress.

I was now thirteen years old and beginning to create a definite sense of personal style. The daisy period of fashion had arrived. Anything with daises won my approval. My new plastic head clip with a row of pink daisies to hold my hair in place was so popular. The white straw Easter hat I purchased with baby-sitting money featured a strip of daisies decorating the grosgrain ribbon around the base of the crown. On a lazy late summer afternoon Mary, Lianne, Patty, and I could be found picking daisies in the field behind Dr. Platt's house. We made pretty necklaces and never failed to play the game *He loves me, He loves me not*, pulling off each long, delicate, white petal one by one, hoping for the best.

Rejecting a new dress adorned with this favorite flower bordered on the implausible. The clerk folded tissue paper around the unwanted item and placed it in a garment box. We all drove back to Riverside.

"What do you think of my dress, Mom?"

"It doesn't look like you, Anita."

"It is ugly, Mom: too fancy and too lacy."

"Then why did you buy it? Don't you know better than that?"

"Mrs. Overdeep is hard to say no to. She is so nice."

"You are going to have to learn to speak your mind," advised my mother.

The discussion went no further, but right then a personal plan of action began to formulate in my head.

I needed to exchange that dreadful dress. A return trip to the New York Lace department store tomorrow was imperative. My new, fat-tire Columbia bike afforded the only mode of transportation for that long twelve-mile ride back to Pawtucket. Carrying the box, tissue paper, sales slip, as well as the dress, I went up to my bedroom and repackaged my purchase.

The next morning after breakfast Mary charged out the back door so as not to be late for her job at the playground. My mother and three-year-old little sister, Alicia, readied themselves for Girl Scout day camp. Mrs. Haskins, my former Brownie leader, arrived at our house to pick them up to drive the few miles to the day camp. It was held in a hilly patch of woods adjacent to the busy Veterans Memorial Parkway. Mrs. Haskins and my mother* were good friends and long-time Girl Scout leaders who took on the task of directing day camp for two weeks each summer. Waiting at the top of the stairs, I heard Mrs. Haskins' old car make its noisy departure; the signal to begin my journey.

The Christmas I received my new fat-tire Columbia bike

227

Since this remained a shopping expedition, wearing a dress seemed like the correct attire. My dad had already left for work and it was my responsibility to lock up. The secret shingle on the side of our house, when lifted, allowed the key to release and drop on to the ground. After securing the back door and returning the key to its proper place I walked to the garage and fetched my bike. The dress box did not fit tight and snug in the wire basket, but it appeared secure enough for the trip.

I had my travels mapped out in my head and knew my way only as far as my Aunt Kay's. She lived in Rumford and Pawtucket was the next town over. Rumford was familiar, but Pawtucket was foreign territory. Stopping at my aunt's house for directions was vital.

The first few miles of my journey out of Riverside ran along a busy street. The high, narrow sidewalk caused the passing cars to come uncomfortably close. Riding my bike demanded my total attention. I could not allow myself to be distracted by the view of Narragansett Bay in the distance.

A few miles further at a fork in the road, I turned right in the direction of Rumford. The cars going left on to Veterans' Memorial Parkway took much of the traffic heading into Providence. I breathed a sigh of relief.

Familiar landmarks were comforting: Kent Heights water tower, Wampanoag Trail, Warren Avenue, Taunton Avenue, and a few signs to nearby Seekonk, Massachusetts. The Newman Congregational Church, a Rumford town landmark, signaled that Aunt Kay's house was just a short distance down the road. Noticing a plaque on the front lawn of the church, I hopped off my bike to read it. The pristine white house of worship with its squared-off steeple noted that it was built in 1810 for a congregation that was first established in 1643. Our family had driven by this sign countless times but never stopped to read it.

Lucky for me, Aunt Kay was home. For some reason she did not think it strange for her young niece to be biking all this distance alone into unknown territory. Like some of her sisters, she had a wanderlust and thought people, both children and adults, should possess the same curiosity to learn and experience new things. Aunt Kay gave me something to eat and drink and vague directions to Pawtucket's shopping district.

"Anita, go down Ferris Avenue past the rifle range and take a right when you get to Newport Avenue. Be careful and look for the signs to the Slater Mill**. The department store is near the Blackstone River bridge and the mill."

Newport Avenue, a main thoroughfare, was crammed with small businesses, houses, car repair shops, buildings of all sorts, pedestrians, and kids on bikes. Peddling past the Slater Park Zoo, I remembered that our family had visited there once or twice. It would have been fun to ride in through the gates, but not today.

Cars and trucks were everywhere. I kept moving along, remembering Aunt Kay's words of caution. Signs advertising the Slater Mill began to pop up, all directing me to the left. Leaving Newport Avenue behind and heading into strange neighborhoods made me uneasy. The only reassurance came each time signs advertising Slater Mill or the Pawtucket shopping district appeared on a sign post or the side of a building.

The businesses started to fade and, with each ensuing block, old rundown houses lining street after street became the norm. Peddling faster, I managed to kept my mounting fear in check.

A housing project to the right caught my attention. There were several long, one-story buildings lined up like cars in a parking lot. The surrounding yards were strewn with trash and old tricycles and bikes. Children played on a flat, dusty, dirt area mostly devoid of grass. I slowed down, hoping no one noticed me gawking, knowing all along it was wrong.

"Maybe the kids playing won't notice me staring at them or see my clean dress and shiny blue bike," I thought.

I moved on, ashamed, reflecting on my actions.

Landmarks remembered from yesterday's trip came in quick succession. The shopping district and the New York Lace department store suddenly came into view.

People were crowded near the entrance waiting for the bus. It occurred to me that my bike could be in danger of being stolen if left unattended. An older man, appearing relaxed and leaning against the building at the store's entrance, caught my attention. Without giving it any thought, I asked if he would watch my bike.

"It will take only a minute. My dress needs to be exchanged."

He smiled and said yes.

"Thank you. I will be right back."

The daisy dress, still hanging on the rack, fortunately did not require any additional money, a factor I had not given the slightest consideration. Having made my even exchange, I dashed out the front store door.

The bike watcher was still standing in the warm sunshine with my bike in front of him. Relieved to see my bike, I thanked the man again and hoped his agreeing to guard my bike did not cause him to miss his bus.

For some reason the return trip did not make me apprehensive or confused concerning directions. A stop at Aunt Kay's wasn't necessary. Wanting to get home forced me to ride faster, but first I needed to stop at Girl Scout day camp to surprise my mother. A quick U-turn on to Veterans' Memorial Parkway soon landed me at the entrance to the Girl Scout day camp.

Alicia waved and called out to me. As usual, when my little sister attended day camp she wore a clothesline around her waist secured to a tree with a long tether in between. My mother wouldn't chance Alicia wandering out to Veterans' Memorial Parkway when her attention was diverted assisting campers. Alicia adapted to her restraints and played alongside everyone else, but with considerably less freedom.

Camp was almost over for the day and my mother had several girls gathered around while she tried to teach them the proper way to fold the American flag.

She wondered aloud why I had come all this way riding my bike in a dress. I gave her a brief explanation of my tale. She was getting used to my adventures and not surprised at what I had done. Maybe she felt confident that this ride would never be repeated.

My mother looked at me and just shook her head and smiled.

"Hurry along. I'll see you when you get home. You can try on the dress for me. I am sure it is lovely. I know how much you like daisies."

I had peddled my not-so-speedy balloon-tire bike a total of 24 miles (round trip) to buy my handsome, stylish, daisy dress.

Worth every mile.

Following my mother's retirement after many years as a Girl Scout leader and serving on several scout committees, she was awarded the Thank You Badge: *the highest award presented to an adult Girl Scout volunteer at that time. She was very proud of it and gifted it to Mrs. Haskins a short time prior to her death in 1972.*

**Slater Mill, Pawtucket, Rhode Island, 1793: An historic textile mill on the Blackstone River modeled after the spinning mills in England. It was the first water-powered spinning mill in North America.*

IN VOGUE

Rainy Day Gear

These raincoats were all the rage when I was in the sixth grade. They were made of heavy, cotton gabardine, complete with a matching hood lined with plaid taffeta.

I was the only one of my friends who had an ugly hood lining. The colors of purple, orange, and navy did not suit my taste. I wanted a Scottish plaid of some sort. A Black Watch plaid would have been perfect.

I kept my hood on my head even when the rain had ceased. Eventually, I slipped it off and folded the hood in such a way that the offensive plaid stayed concealed.

But all was not lost. A few years later my mother bought me a very stylish in-vogue red oilcloth slicker with a matching fisherman's hat. I was the first person in my ninth grade class to have one. I loved this rain gear and wore it even when the weather forecast predicted only the slightest chance of inclement weather.

THE MONKEY LADY
The Waiting Game

The word flew around our small neighborhood with the speed of a summer brush fire.

"Mrs. Harris is bringing her monkey out to play this afternoon."

Kids scattered, ran home for lunch, and in no time were sitting lined up in a single row along the embankment across the street from the monkey's home.

Mrs. Harris, the Monkey Lady, lived right up the lane from us. Her white clapboard house with contrasting black shutters on each window, was one of the most unusual and attractive houses in the neighborhood. All the homes in our little community faced the road, but hers sat sideways on a double lot. A screened-in porch ran along the entire east side of the house that must have made for a cheery place for her to sit in the morning sunshine.

Mrs. Harris lived on the corner of Dyer Avenue and Harris Street which made me wonder if she was related to a Civil War soldier, since some of the streets in our section of town were named to honor those warriors. Several were buried in the historic Little Neck Cemetery located along Bullocks Cove.

She did not look any different from other mothers in the neighborhood, except older and with grey hair. Our mothers had children entrusted to their care, but Mrs. Harris had a single little monkey to attend to.

I don't know who started the rumor that her unusual pet would be making an appearance, but it may have been Dickie Blake, her next-door neighbor. We never took the chance that this could be false information since missing such a momentous event was out of the question. We feared that the opportunity may never present itself again.

The neighborhood kids sat on the grass watching and waiting. We soon became restless and bored. Some began to make slingshots out of plantain weeds and fired them at unsuspecting targets. A minor boys' wrestling match sometimes ensued but, for the most part, we tried to be on our best behavior, fearing the Monkey Lady would look out the window and see a bunch of hoodlums behaving badly and decide to stay inside.

One of the boys insisted he knew that the Monkey Lady took a bath with her pet on Saturday night. We all loved to hear that story. Sometimes I thought of Mrs. Harris and her monkey when I was having a bath.

Once, out of all the countless times we sat across the street and waited for the monkey to appear, it happened. The Monkey Lady opened the screen door, holding her tiny charge. She held on to the thin leather leash secured around his slender neck. Mrs. Harris carried her small, wiggling monkey with the same loving care that one might coddle a newborn. She walked over to the middle of the side lawn and sat on the grass. The monkey danced and cavorted around her, acting silly and playful.

Mrs. Harris did not speak to us, but she once looked our way and smiled. After a brief time, she retraced her steps and they both vanished into the long, narrow side porch.

We all watched in silence and wonder that day. No one said it, but we all knew. It was worth the many long, endless vigils on the embankment, passing time, waiting for the monkey's arrival.

MRS. VILLENUEVE

And Company

To achieve my objective, I was willing to tolerate the horrific scene that presented itself on the mantel of the Villeneuve's living room fireplace year after year. Enduring this act of personal courage put me one step closer to my sought-after goal: a full day off from school to participate at a Mass said by the bishop at the Catholic cathedral in Providence.

I counted on Mrs. Villeneuve and other kind neighbors to purchase newspaper subscriptions to win this prize. She never refused my annual solicitation of a subscription to the Catholic diocesan newspaper, *The Providence Visitor.*

She and her family lived on the very fringe of our neighborhood, so I did not know them very well. I passed by their well-kept house and yard each day on my way to school. Mrs. Villeneuve lived with her husband and two almost adult children. She wore clothes nicer than a normal house dress on her short, sturdy, broad frame. Mr. Villeneuve, a well-groomed slim man, seemed small in contrast to his wife's imposing physical appearance.

I did win the subscription contest for three years: two second places and I came in first in eighth grade. These selling feats guaranteed a trip into Providence with several other students. No parent or teacher accompanied this group of energetic, untethered, sixth, seventh, and eighth graders. We were on our own and aching for adventure.

The day of freedom could not come soon enough. Taking the early bus guaranteed an on-time arrival. The six of us walked through the shopping district and proceeded to hike up the hill toward the cathedral to join the other diocesan winners. We entered the cathedral and took our seats on one of the many polished dark wood pews.

Bishop Russell J. McVinney, the Bishop of Providence, greeted us in his flowing, elaborately embellished robes. A tall slender pointy hat balanced precariously on his dense crop of white hair.

Just prior to the conclusion of the service, one of the bishop's aides directed the students to form a line leading up the center aisle. The bishop sat waiting in an ornate chair just inside the open communion railing. We approached and one by one knelt in front of him. He lifted his left hand. On that signal each young recipient in turn leaned forward and kissed his ring: a huge, sparkling, extraordinary red ruby resting atop a fancy engraved gold setting.

The Mass always ran longer than our restless bodies could barely endure. A few of us waited until all the students filed out of the cathedral. We then darted up the spiral stairs to the choir loft that overlooked the cavernous empty cathedral. We leaned over the railing and called to the three better-behaved St. Brendan's students below. We examined every secret nook in the infinite eves surrounding the loft. Almost as if on cue we descended the stairs, ran down the hill to the White Tower for lunch, and finished off our day of independence with a movie at the Majestic theater.

These thoughts of fun and freedom floated and bounced around in my head as I stood ringing the bell on the steps of the Villeneuve's front door.

In time, Mrs. Villeneuve opened the door. I did not have to explain my visit. She knew why I was there since I only came to call once a year.

"Why hello, Anita, or are you Mary? You two look so much alike. I can never tell you apart."

Mary and I did not look alike, but I politely nodded my head in agreement.

"I'm Anita."

"Come in, my dear. Go right in the living room and have a seat. My purse is upstairs."

I lowered myself into a dark upholstered chair. It made no difference where I sat since all the furniture faced in the direction of the fireplace. I cast my eyes down, but only for a moment. The temptation was too great. Like a puppet with body parts attached to strings, I tilted my head back and looked up. To my repulsion and insatiable curiosity, I saw it still residing on the fireplace mantel.

A tall translucent circular vase, filled to the brim with formaldehyde, held the lifeless body of a large murky brown snake curled around and around taking up the entire jar. The snake's mouth, wide open, held a frog partially imprisoned in the its grip. The frog's legs, spread-eagled, exhibited a clear element of surprise even in death. I could almost hear the frog yelling,

"Hey, let go! Get me out of here!"

I was so intent at the vision before me I did not hear Mrs. Villeneuve enter the room. I jerked my body around attempting to appear calm and nonchalant.

Every year I heard the same explanation.

"Oh, Anita, my Rene caught the snake devouring that frog down at the brook. Isn't it interesting?"

"Yes, Mrs. Villeneuve, it is."

I wanted to say what was going through my head, but I did not.

Rene could have left the snake alone and let it do what snakes do: eat frogs. Then there would be one dead animal, not two. Wasn't it mean-spirited to bring a live snake home with a wiggling meal hanging out of its mouth? The biggest question of all: why did Mrs. Villeneuve use it as home décor for all the world to see?

No frog-eating snake on our mantel. We had a mint green ceramic deer with pointed ears holding vines cascading down the front of the fireplace. On the opposite side, another ceramic vase, in the shape of a ram with, yes, a snake plant growing out of an opening in its back. These two decorations seemed normal to me.

*Me on my First Communion day
standing in front of the
snake plant on the fireplace mantel*

I thanked Mrs. Villeneuve and put the money in my envelope, walked down her front steps, turned the corner, and headed back up Harris Street.

I bolted into the kitchen. My mother, standing in front of the stove, had just finished preparing dinner.

"Hey, Mom, Mrs. Villeneuve still has that snake swallowing a frog on her fireplace mantel. It hasn't rotted yet. It is so weird and ugly. I really didn't want to look at it, but I can't resist. It's so disgusting. I can't wait to tell Mary and Alicia about the gross stuff in the jar."

"Anita, they have all heard it before. You know how Mary hates talking about snakes and your vivid account may upset your little sister. Yes, it is a very unusual decoration. I'm amazed it is still holding up. Dinner is just about ready. Please go find Mary and Alicia and tell them it is time to eat, but first wash your hands."

I saw my mother smile, shake her head, and glance at the ceiling. Exhibiting great restraint during our evening meal was difficult, but I conformed to my mother's wise counsel.

AGATE BAGGET
Bag of Gold

My agate bagget contained all my precious glass marbles. Mary and our best friend, Lianne Good, also had an agate bagget. My mother sewed all three rectangular, drawstring bags for us while we stood next to her sewing machine waiting, impatiently, for our new containers to be completed. We all called those bags our agate baggets. My cloth container was constructed from the sewing scraps of a favorite, flowered, brown, cotton dress featuring bouquets of small, pink roses scattered here and there. Unlike the girls, the neighborhood boys never considered using anything that came dangerously close to resembling a girl's purse. They carried their agates loose, deep in the pockets of their shapeless dungarees or swishy corduroy knickers.

Agates or marbles had value. The most desirable, the Queenies, were infused with variegated, vivid colors. The smaller ones, similar in design, were of the everyday variety and played most often. Sometimes I emptied my bag and spilled all its contents on the living room rug lining them up in a row straight as a ruler. I counted them, admiring my bounty as if they were precious gemstones. I wanted to get to know them well, since sometimes mine resembled those owned by my friends.

When not in use, I hung my flowered bag on a hook next to the dry mop in the cleaning closet, located right behind the kitchen stove. Sometimes, the bag hung limp with its sagging form exposing the shapes of only a few agates. This called for a game: a time to win back my loot.

We had the best playing surface in the entire neighborhood. My father designed and built a screened-in summer porch that he attached along the entire west side of the garage. At the first sighting of a mosquito, he would carry the screens from their winter storage spot and attach each one in its proper place. The room had a hard dirt floor that received an occasional flattening by my dad using his homemade cement roller. A few Herculean pushes resulted in a surface as level and smooth as the lanes down at the Riverside Bowling Alley.

Whoever had the best hard rubber or leather heels on their shoes earned the task of turning around and around, heel to the ground, grinding a hole deep enough for the marbles to roll into. Too shallow a depression resulted in the agates rolling down one side and out the other. We patted and re-patted the area, attempting to achieve perfection, usually with all players yelling at once, giving advice.

"That hole is uneven."

"Make it deeper. The agates are gonna roll out the other side."

"Hey, your shoes aren't good enough, let Pee Wee dig it. He has leather heals."

This banter kept up until most everyone agreed that the hole was ready for play.

The rules were simple. A line drawn in the dirt with a stick, at an agreed-upon distance from the hole, determined the starting line of play. The players decided on the number of agates and people to comprise a game. We took turns and had teams, each of us using only one index finger to propel the agates on their intended journey. The player who got all his or her own agates into the hole first claimed the pieces played. Sometimes fights would ensue and the participants would grab their agates and disperse before the game was complete.

"Come on. Let's keep playing. Don't quit," chimed a player, trying to persuade someone huffing and heading out the screen door.

We had some good players in the neighborhood. They were usually the boys. Fuffa played for the kill. He took chances. If his winnings were big, he would walk away at the end of play and not reappear for weeks. Pee Wee intimidated everyone. Like a geometry problem waiting to be solved, Pee Wee knew how to figure angles for the best shot. He had an edge, but we played with him just the same.

I played mostly with Lianne and my sister, Mary. Lianne loved to compete in anything and wanted to win as much as I did. She would argue over the positioning of the agates and spend long periods of time kneeling with her nose almost hitting the ground smoothing the dirt. After a morning of play, Lianne often returned for a rematch in the afternoon, especially if she had lost and her agate bagget was almost empty.

Mary and I had our own rules. I would play the big ones, my Queenies, with her. These were so valuable that I trusted them only with my sister. If Mary won one of my large beauties, I knew that negotiations followed play. A trade taking on her Saturday chores in exchange for getting my Queenies returned seemed a fair deal.

I often misplaced things, but never my agate bagget. Of all areas in the house the cleaning supply closet appeared to be the safest hiding place for my treasures. In time, I grew up and my interest in playing agates waned. Sometimes I noticed a dust cloth draped over my brown flowered bag. I considered this an added measure of protection. Over the years I forgot about agates and childhood games. Other activities became important in my life, none more so, at age sixteen, than driving the family car.

One day, walking past the cleaning closet, I remembered my agates. I opened the door to check on them. I wanted to feel their cool, smooth surfaces again and to take pleasure in listening to the sound of their click-clack as I stirred them in the bag with the tips of my fingers.

The hooks were full. I noticed a worn feather duster, the dry mop in its usual place, a faded blue umbrella, a long grey extension attachment for the Electrolux vacuum cleaner draped over a hook, but not my agate bagget. I then took on the task of emptying the entire closet.

My little brown bag was nowhere to be found. I asked my mother about its whereabouts. She claimed to have not seen it in years. I said nothing. I knew. Long ago, I became familiar with my mother's tossing-out habits.

I recall her saying, "If you don't use something within a year, it is time to get rid of it."

I felt sad, empty, misunderstood, and alone. Didn't my mother know how much my agate bagget meant to me? I had intended to keep it forever, but neglected to tell anyone.

My father entered the kitchen, taking a break from a woodworking project in the basement. I brightened, forgetting about my agates, my tormented soul, my lost youth. I walked over to him and smiled my best smile.

"Hey Dad, mind if I drive over to Barbara's before supper? It's my turn to set the table so I won't be long. I'll be back on time".

"No" was not an operative word with my dad concerning his three daughters. He trusted us, wanted to make us happy, and never liked being the bad guy.

He smiled, slipped his hand into his brown trouser pants pocket and pulled out the car keys.

"Here. Catch."

Me polishing the family car

IN VOGUE

Thank You, Alicia

My white bouffant toile skirt, black velvet top, and silver-strap high heels exemplified fashion perfection.

My mother sewed the skirt for me using two layers of net

fabric. Three would have been ideal, but a few crinoline petticoats underneath did an excellent job of extending the skirt out as far as physically possible.

I borrowed the handsome, bare-sleeve velvet top from my sister Mary's best friend, Margaret. Girls borrowed clothes from one another back then.

My little sister, Alicia, followed me around while I primped myself for the school Christmas dance. She stood by my side as I gazed at myself using the full-length mirror in my parents' bedroom. She balanced a tray containing eye shadow, mascara, lipstick, powder, flower earrings, and silver sparkle for my hair. Alicia handed them to me per my request and continued to follow me, like a dutiful little puppy, until the job was complete and I no longer needed her faithful service.

I was very happy and grateful to have Alicia assisting me. She was a wonderful helper.

LOVE LOST

Pitter-Patter

The red numeral blinked on the telephone. One message. I pressed the button.

"Nita, this is Nancy, I hate to be a bearer of bad news, but Fuffa Dubois died yesterday. I'll call you tomorrow."

Fuffa Dubois (Richard) and Pee Wee Brown (Elwood) were the two most important boys in our neighborhood. Pee Wee's nickname made sense because he was small for his age, but Fuffa's name remained a total mystery, like himself. The six neighborhood girls: Nancy, Lianne, Dotty, Patty, Mary, and me considered two boys and six girls a fine balance.

Top (l-r): Dottie, Nancy, Patty
Bottom (l-r): Me, Lianne, Mary

The eight of us were always on the ready for a new adventure. We climbed apple trees in Pee Wee's backyard, tramped through the mud down at the swamp, constructed wobbly rock bridges across the brook, and made dams in a futile attempt to bring the water to a standstill from the feeder pond upstream.

A favorite activity involved looking for big, square-shelled box turtles. If we were lucky enough to locate two, we had a turtle race. Someone took a stick and drew a line in the hard-packed dirt path that divided the swamp. There was lots of yelling, but sometimes the turtles would not head in the direction of the finish line, as we naively thought they would, but slowly retreated in the direction of the water. We ate the peppery watercress that clung to the sides of the embankment and did just about anything that garnered our imagination. The main objective in our young lives was to play and have fun.

The four years difference in age between Fuffa and me did not matter. I loved my neighborhood friend in my childlike way. I watched him ride his bike past my house going to hang out with Pee Wee. I monitored him from my backyard, concealing myself behind the sheets fluttering in the breeze on our clothesline. I strained my eyes and peered beyond his grandfather's two corn fields, observing him take off on his bike in such a hurry that the racoon tail attached to the rear fender flew out straight. Fuffa's rapid departure was often followed by a high pitched, "Rich-Chard, Rich-Chard," sung by his grandmother standing in the driveway. Her bird-like call did not merit his return.

Fuffa, a slim boy of average height, olive complexion, neatly combed light brown hair, and a sly smile caused my heart to flutter. He appeared spotless in appearance due to the undivided attention of his grandmother. He lived with his grandparents, Grandmother and Grandfather Gill. His father, a career Air Force man, visited periodically. On these trips back, Mr. Dubois always arrived with an expensive gift for his young son: a favorite being a brown leather bomber jacket with the official Air Force insignia embroidered on the front. Fuffa wore it so much that the leather began to develop fine wrinkles leading one to imagine that Mr. Dubois' young son might have been a member of the Air Force too. We never knew anything about his mother, nor did we inquire.

I called my sister, Mary, to inform her of our friend's death.

"Mary, what do you remember about Fuffa?" I asked.

"I loved the rope swing that we had behind Mr. Daniel's wood shop, you know, that long building next to where we played bordering the swamp down by the brook. Fuffa climbed up a tall tree and attached a long rope. We would grab the rope, secure our feet against the bottom knot and hold on for dear life. With a giant push from someone you sailed out over the embankment. The swamp and briar patches waited below if you lost your grip. It was dangerous and hard to hold on, but that is what made it so much fun."

We put on circus shows in the Brown's side yard. Fuffa had two sets of real Joe Palooka leather boxing gloves. He and Pee Wee danced around inside the ring swinging wildly at each other enclosed in a homemade boxing arena that we had constructed using four wooden poles and some rope. The girls stood on the periphery, out of harm's way, and cheered them on.

One day we decided to dig a foxhole in the far end of Pee Wee's yard. The area we lived in was once an apple orchard with several of the trees still standing. It was a good spot to carry on secret projects since the dense leaf cover shielded us from view.

Some of us went home and fetched shovels and we took turns digging. When the team effort met with the boys' approval, the girls put their shovels aside, but Pee Wee and Fuffa dug further, branching out and making more underground rooms off the main one. When they thought it looked about perfect, everyone climbed down and crowded into the dark, dank, claustrophobic spaces. For one split second we were all quiet. The realization that a cave-in was a distinct possibility dawned on everyone in that moment. Fuffa and Pee Wee gave the orders to climb out and not to walk on the grass roof above the subterranean cave. We did as we were told and averted possible disaster. The boys filled in the cave with dirt and everyone took their shovels and went home.

Cowboys and Indians occupied much of our time. The cowboys would yell, "Giddy-up" to their imaginary horses and the Indians crept around making sounds to scare the cowboys by putting a hand over their mouths and emitting a low sound warning the opponent they were on the prowl. The object was to hit your adversary with pretend arrows. The cry of *I got you* meant you were dead and had to fall to the ground and lay perfectly still.

What I liked best about this game was that Fuffa and I were the only Indians. His headdress, a gift from his father, was trimmed with tall,

Top row (l-r): Nancy, Mary, Patty
Bottom row (l-r): Fuffa, and me

straight feathers attached to a leather band around his head. Tassels, festooned with fluffy white feathers, hung down on either side of his face, making him appear as a genuine, authentic Indian. This was in sharp contrast to mine made from a cloth strip, decorated with crayon, and adorned with one single feather at the back of my head. The simplicity of my homemade headdress was of little importance since being an Indian meant Fuffa and I were partners for as long as the game lasted.

As he got older, Fuffa drifted away from the neighbor kids. He played baseball on the Riverside Junior High School team. Sometimes I would walk over to the recreation field and watch a few innings. I never paid attention to the plays, the score, or what school happened to be the opposing team. The player covering second base was my only interest. Never once did Fuffa glance in my direction. He loved baseball and we knew he was a Yankee fan so Mary and I became Yankee fans.

My sister and I stayed overnight at the Gill's home when our grandmother died. We slept in a room beyond Fuffa's bedroom on the second floor that had two single beds and was used as storage space. A curtained doorway separated his room from ours. We listened, but never heard a squeak from his bed, a snore, or a cough. When Mrs. Gill called us to breakfast, we had to walk through his room to reach the stairs. The small, tidy bedroom appeared unused and to our dismay, no Fuffa. He had vanished without a trace, but we both knew that his elusiveness was all part of our juvenile attraction to him.

•　•　•　•　•

In June 2015, the now grown-up neighborhood girlfriends met for lunch at the Old Grist Mill, a landmark restaurant on the Rhode Island-Massachusetts line. Nancy stopped en route from New Hampshire to Florida, Lianne traveled from Houston, Patty and Mary came from Rehoboth and Boston, Massachusetts, Dottie drove up from nearby

Riverside, and I flew in from Buffalo. As we all dined on lobster rolls, our conversation, time and again, centered on our growing-up years and how fortunate we were to have experienced such happy childhoods. We began to talk about the *boys*. Nancy laughed and said, "I loved Fuffa." Then Patty chimed in, "Hey, so did I." Dottie quietly summed it up, "We were all in love with Fuffa."

Mary and I could not believe what we had just heard. All these years we considered that the fascination and crush we both had on Fuffa represented a simple sister rivalry vying for a smile or a nod of recognition from this quiet, unassuming kid. Now, decades later, we learned that our competition encompassed the six of us, the entire girl population of our neighborhood, as his adoring fans.

Fuffa died a year following the girls' neighborhood reunion. In retrospect I wished now we had extended an invitation to our handsome, quiet, retiring childhood lost love, but knowing his practice of avoidance and dodging attention, he may have been difficult to locate. To compound things, there was always an outside chance that our elusive friend's telephone number may not have been listed.

CHARLIE GAMAGE AND NELLIE

Neighborhood Farm

I wasn't sure just how to pronounce the word OshKosh, but Mr. Gamage, the only farmer in the neighborhood, wore this style of denim overalls with one wide strap over each shoulder every day.

I thought Mr. Gamage, a short man with an enormous belly, didn't require shoulder straps on his bib overalls to keep them from losing their grip. His girth did a fine job of keeping everything in place.

Mr. Gamage, known around town as Charlie, lived in a large two-story farmhouse situated on a rise, set back from the sidewalk by a cement wall. A lengthy screened-in porch ran along the entire front of the house. The Gamage house was in sharp contrast to their neighbors, the Villeneuves, who resided across the street in a trim two-story colonial home.

A driveway split the farm property in two. The small barn to the left provided Nellie, his hefty work horse, a comfortable place to reside. Nellie sported a long, white, bushy mane and a shaggy tail that stretched to the ground. Her huge hoofs remained almost hidden under rough, uneven clumps of hair. The barn doors, open during the daytime hours, gave the impression that lots of farming was in progress. Another section of the barn continued on behind their house. This end of the barn had a hay loft on the second floor with doors always ajar. It appeared untidy. Hay spilled out on to the ground below, affording a continual feast for the free-roaming chickens. Nellie, chickens, dogs, and cats comprised the entire animal kingdom at the Gamage farm.

I often paused as I passed the farm on my way to and from elementary school, but it was difficult to spot any major goings-on. I liked to imagine that some fat, pink pigs and maybe a goat or two were in residence, but things stayed the same.

I could always count on Mr. and Mrs. Gamage to be rocking in their chairs, all in a straight line facing the street on the front porch, as I walked by their farm in the late afternoon. A third person, who I imagined to be Mrs. Gamage's sister, sat to her left, also rocking. They waved and I returned their greeting. I don't recall ever saying anything, just a friendly wave.

Things were different when my little sister, Alicia, was old enough to go to school. She took the same route as I once did.

"Hey, is your mother still feeding you fertilizer?" Mr. Gamage invariably shouted down to Alicia as she walked by.

Alicia, taller than any of her friends and self-conscious about her height, didn't care for his daily holler. Feeling hurt and wanting to cry following his comments, she put on a brave face and waved back to the rocking trio.

It was a lucky day if I happened to be home when Mr. Gamage arrived with Nellie to plow Mr. Gill's land for the spring planting of his two gardens located adjacent to our property. The huge horse

Riverside's Memorial Day Parade: Alicia is carrying the American flag.

clopped down the street with Mr. Gamage sitting slumped forward on a worn wooden seat atop a platform behind Nellie. He held on to the oily leather reins guiding his faithful horse in the right direction. A circular plow and long rake, raised high, were attached to the rear of the wagon preventing the equipment from scraping along the road.

Once in the field, Mr. Gamage released the gears and the plow dropped to the ground. He snapped the leather reins while he made clicking sounds with his mouth. Nellie ambled forward obeying her master's commands. The metal discs dug into soil turning the dried grasses over and bringing up smooth, silky, heavy soil, dark and rich. The straight, wide cylindrical rows of churned dirt first appeared tight and solid, but in time they cracked and broke apart. With the rough plowing complete he then hoisted the plow and lowered the formidable rake. Nellie moseyed forward, dragging this second piece of equipment along the uneven ground. Mr. Gamage kept up this process until he deemed it was smooth enough for Mr. Gill to begin his spring planting.

I sat on the side embankment of my yard, watching with undivided attention. I, too, departed when they completed their task and the farmer and his horse vanished around the corner on to Harris Street heading back to their Turner Avenue farm.

One day Mr. Gill approached my mother and father and asked them if they would like to purchase the lot closest to our house for $300. I could not believe our good fortune. I saw my future dancing before my eyes. I would become the most popular kid in the neighborhood. I imagined forts, a ball field, and a smooth platform for a bigger and better area to roll agates. Maybe my father would even construct a playhouse.

Never wanting to disappoint his girls, my father was an easy "yes." My mother, on the other hand, envisioned a future of planting beans, tomatoes, corn, and beets in the hot and humid weather. Canning the bounty would follow. She won out in the end and the land did not become ours. Neighbors who lived on the main road bought the lot and planned to build a house and move around the corner to the suburbs. They planted a formal flower garden of mostly gladiolus and a trellis laden with pink roses that bloomed in profusion each June. It remained this way for a few years until one day I heard a commotion outside the dining room window.

Mr. Gamage and Nellie were preparing to dig a foundation hole so that our neighbors, the Romans, could build their house. This time a large, cumbersome metal scoop hit the ground with a resounding thud. Mr. Gamage prodded Nellie along. The horse seemed to struggle under the weight of the shovel. It took two days for the hole to be completed. Again, I sat on the lawn and watched the depression get deeper and deeper, but this time with a heavy heart. I knew our lives were about to change.

Mr. and Mrs. Roman built their house: a small, one-story, pretty, cedar-shingled home with aqua shutters. I did not like people living so close. If I stood at the very end of the dining room windows, I could watch Mrs. Roman washing dishes. I missed the cornfields.

By the ninth grade I no longer walked by the sole neighborhood farm. My long hike to Riverside Junior High School took me along Burnside Avenue and down the dirt path to the swamp, over the wooden bridge at the brook, and eventually to school. I could see the Gamage's cement wall in the distance as I turned right on to Burnside Avenue, but I was no longer fascinated by their farm. I had other things on my teenage mind.

I stopped by my best friend, Nancy's, home and we walked together hoping, if we kept the right pace, we might meet up with (handsome) Walter Crocker and (very smart and funny) Earl Briden. Luck was often on our side and the four of us laughed and flirted as we trudged up the hill to junior high.

Those late spring days of idling on the embankment watching Mr. Gamage and Nellie plow the cornfield each year were, like my childhood, now a thing of the past.

•   •   •   •   •